A BIRDWATCHI

CRETE

STEPHANIE COGHLAN

ARLEQUIN

ISBN 1 900159 10 4

First published 1996

Arlequin Press, 26 Broomfield Road, Chelmsford, Essex CM1 1SW
Telephone: 01245 267771
© Stephanie Coghlan

A catalogue record for this book is available.

CONTENTS

PREFACE to 4th EDITION

This guide began life as "Easter Birdwatching in Crete" and then grew to be "Birdwatching in Crete" which ran to three editions. Now it is expanding and metamophosing with additional site information and a review of the status of the birds on Crete plus a revised checklist into "A Birdwatcher's Guide to Crete".

Following further visits to the island of Crete and in response to the many people who have written to me with additional information about the birds they have seen and areas which they have visited much of the guide has been rewritten.

The success of plans to protect the Almyros marsh at Agios Nikolaos and the Aposelemis river at Gouves and other sites have waxed and waned. So despite an EU grant and the hard work of Anne Cryer and Doug Ireland and many others there are still no fully protected sites on the island apart from the Samaria Gorge, although many areas are displaying no hunting signs, sadly often ignored judging by the cartridge cases lying about.

Please help us to promote conservation on the island by acting as an ambassador for birdwatching throughout your visit to Crete.

ACKNOWLEDGMENTS

Many thanks to the numerous people who have submitted records, written about their visits to Crete, and have offered encouragement for all the editions of this booklet. There are too many to mention by name but without them this edition would not be so complete.

Particular thanks to Jim Coghlan for his support and encouragement and to Denis Townsend for his continued work in helping compile the Annual Reports and the 1986-1995 Survey, and also to John & Chris Henshall for their dedicated work in compiling records, since they moved to live permanently on the island.

Finally many thanks to Stella & Stelios Zourarakis of Lyttos Travels on Crete and to Mollie Brown and Ron Heaps for their hospitality and help during reconnaissance trips.

Thanks also to Ian Rutherford for his assistance with the butterfly records.

INTRODUCTION

Crete lies on the 35° latitude in the southern Mediterranean. It is about 160 miles or 250 km long and is nearly 42 miles or 60 km at its widest point. It is situated about 200 miles from the coasts of North Africa, Asia, and Europe, and these continents have influenced its history and its wildlife. As a large island separated early in its history, a wealth of endemic plants have evolved, other endemics are the Cretan spiny mouse, and some local varieties of butterflies.

Crete is the fifth largest island in the Mediterranean and is very mountainous. There are three mountain ranges in the main part of the island; the White Mountains in the west, the Idha Mountains in the centre, of which the peak Psiloritis, is the highest on the island(2,456m), the Dikti Mountains to the east of Heraklion and a fourth lower range to the east behind Sitia. Many of the mountains are cut by impressive gorges of which the most well known is the Samaria Gorge in the south west. From the birdwatcher's point of view these gorges offer breeding areas for Griffon Vultures and Lammergeier and Blue Rock Thrush as well as good observation points.

In the early Spring there are many resident and breeding migrants on the island and a wide variety of migrants are streaming through from Africa on their way north. Autumn is also a challenging time for identification but at any time, apart from the very hot months of July and August, Crete offers a great deal to the birdwatcher, botanist and general naturalist, as well as the archaeologist, sun worshipper and relaxed tourist.

AREAS TO STAY
NORTH COAST
The main communication route and the largest towns are along the north coast. Tourism has naturally grown up around these centres and working from west to east Chania, Rethymnon, Heraklion and Aghios Nikolaos are the main areas where people stay. Despite the increasing size of the towns and the growing number of hotels the island still has plenty to offer the birdwatcher and naturalist.

The north west has some interesting river mouths and the fresh water marsh at Georgioupolis would make a good base. Alternatively Rethymnon and Chania or Kastelli Kissamou could be used as centres for reaching the north west and the far west.

The largest number of hotels are on the north east coast, immediately east and to the west of Heraklion. Beaches on this coast are not very good, but there are several good birding spots near Hersonissos, and Aghios Nikolaos.

Malia is now a lively resort, and has attracted some criticism, but it has the best beach on this coast. The marsh here has declined but it and the surrounding area can still be good for birds, especially during migration.

In Spring migrants are present along this north coastal plain and in the olive groves behind, although the carnation farms and coastal meadows are disappearing fast.

The most famous archaeological sites are in the north and centre of the island. Bus services in this area make it easy to reach them, the mountains and the Lassithi Plateau or the south of the island.

SOUTH COAST
Much of the south coast is mountainous, but there are bays and river mouths which provide good beaches. The south east is slightly less mountainous. Ierapetra on the south coast, is near good beaches but does not have a great deal of interest, although a new reservoir on the western edge at Barmiana is a potential new and important site.

Further west along the south coast there are small resorts between Aghia Galini and Chora Sfakion. They are always worth watching for migrants if they have a river or a small marsh. Any patch of water is often a mecca for birds because large stretches of water are rare in Crete.

Plakias is a developing small resort which is good base for the south coast and we have found it an excellent centre for watching migrants and birds of prey. For the general naturalist the area is also good for flowers and butterflies.

Further west Frangocastello, Chora Sfakion, Agia Roumeli, Sougia and Paleochora all offer bases from which to explore. Of these latter places Chora Sfakion and Paleochora have medium to small hotels, while the accommodation offered at the other small resorts is village rooms and tavernas.

EAST COAST
The east coast is very beautiful but isolated. Sandy beaches are accessible by car over rough roads, although the Palm Grove at Vai now has a good road. Kato Zakro and its gorge offers the main birding interest.

Sitia is a quiet town which could be used as a base for visits to the east coast and the Kato Zakro gorge. The harbour and beach are worth regular watching and the Sitia mountains are under recorded. The island's only Egyptian vulture records come from ths area and there must be other secrets to uncover. The islands off the northeast coast are an important Eleonora's falcon colony. A good road leads to the south coast and so Sitia is suitable as a centre for both coasts. The far eastern corner is still unknown, but there is now a small development at Xerokambos, and a river mouth pool, which would be ideal for the really adventurous explorer as this coast is underrecorded at migration time.

WEST COAST

The west coast has small areas of plains backed by hill ridges. This coast is also under explored and under recorded. Falasarna has great potential and the two northern peninsulas are probably migration routes. The far south west is the least developed part of the island but it has some interesting beach and small stream areas waiting to be recorded. There is some taverna accommodation available at places like Falasarna but large hotels and commercial tourism have not yet developed this coast. From Chania day coach tours are now offered to Elaphonisi, once a deserted beach on this coast, so with a developing road system this probably means that larger scale tourism is on its way.

TRAVELLING TO CRETE

Many package tours companies travel to Crete. They offer a wide range of accommodation from Class A to Class C hotels, village rooms, self-catering apartments, villas and fly drive holidays. The season for direct charter flights is April-October. Some of the best companies specialise in Crete only.

Independent travel is not difficult to organise but charter flight tickets only, may be difficult to obtain early in the season.

Fly-Drive Holidays are a good compromise. The two airports are near Heraklion and Chania. The Chania airport is smaller but it is now receiving direct flights from Britain if you are planning to visit the western end of the island, but unfortunately not early in the season.

Flights begin in April to Heraklion, but in May to Chania.

Scheduled flights are also available. All year round the island can be reached via Athens, with connections to Heraklion or Chania with Olympic Airways.

Ferries also arrive daily from mainland Greece.

CAR HIRE

Car hire is very expensive in Crete, booking before departure from Britain can mean a reduced rate but you can easily book a car or jeep in most resorts in Crete by the day or week. It is always wise to check that you have fully comprehensive insurance.

Moped hire is available but it should be considered with caution. Many roads are rough and safety helmets are not always supplied. Again it is advisable to insist on wearing a helmet and to be fully insured, bearing in mind that medical assistance may not be readily available in remoter areas.

Bicycle hire is available in resorts like Malia and Aghios Nikolaos.

BUSES

Buses offer a very good way of getting around. The bus service is efficient and fairly cheap. It is possible to travel over a great deal of the island by local bus with no difficulty. The main bus stations are in Heraklion, Aghios Nikolaos, Rethymnon, and Chania. For planning purposes timetables are available in the Sunflower guides, although they may change from year to year.

If you stop the bus at a bus stop you pay on the bus. If you start from a bus station, buy your ticket, in advance in the booking office, before you board the bus. You will then get a numbered seat.

ROADS

Since our first visits to the island there has been much improvement in Cretan roads but there are still great variations in the road surfaces and these changes are rapid, stretches of improved road, can be followed by a stretch of unimproved and then back to average all within a few yards. It is not an island for fast motoring, although for the determined traveller the main sites can be visited in a fortnight with plenty of time spent in the car. If you can plan two visits to the western and eastern ends of the island, this would allow for a more leisurely exploration of the sites.

The main road is the dual carriageway on the north coast, running from Aghios Nikolaos in the east to Chania in the west. This road has the best surface, it is marked by kilometre posts but the entrances and exits are often illdefined. Many of the roads crossing the island to the south are poor, or even if improved, may have deteriorated due to winter weather or earth movements. Some of the roads marked on maps are still wishful thinking, particularly on the south coast.

SIGNPOSTS

Signposts are improving but are a little thin on the ground in rural areas. The Greek sign is usually followed in 50 metres by a translation, but the spelling may not always agree with the map you may be using.

KILOMETRE SIGNS

The main road and some of the important secondary roads are marked with kilometre posts. On the main road these run from Chania 1 to Ag. Nikolaos 197. Ag. Nikolaos to Sitia begins again at 1. Similarly Chania to Kastelli Kissamou begins again at 1. Where possible I have indicated these kilometre numbers to aid direction to sites.

MAPS

There are Cretan Ordance Survey maps but they are expensive and are not really very helpful. Several maps available from booksellers here are useful but the best maps for passable roads are often those given free when you hire a car. The folding maps in the Sunflower Landscapes series, are some of the best available for accurate road quality.

For placenames the Hildebrand or the Nelles Verlag 1:200,000 Crete are clear.

For walkers there are now a series of 5 larger scale tourist maps with footpaths for the island. They are 1:80,000 scale published by Harms Verlag. Unfortunately they are rather expensive.

SPELLING AND PLACE NAMES

The spelling varies greatly depending on the map or guidebook consulted. As there are similar place names in different regions within Crete this can also be confusing. The names used throughout this guide are those I hope are in general English usage.

River names are also difficult. Potamos is the Greek for river, so a name on a map can be Mylopotamos, or R.Mylo. Accurately naming some of the rivers is not always possible.

Many village names are repeated throughout the island so it is sometimes necessary to check in which district (nome) the village is situated.

The four districts are Chania, Rethymnon, Heraklion and Lassithi.

HOTELS

If you arrive without accommodation there are plenty of hotels, villas, pensions, tavernas, and village rooms available at a wide variety of prices.

All prices in Greece are government controlled. The pricecard is usually behind the door of your room.

CAMP SITES

Campsites are declining on the island. They are mainly on the north coast and are advertised on hoardings on the main coastal highway.

Freelance camping is forbidden throughout Crete.

LANGUAGE

English and German are spoken throughout the island in the tourist areas. In the villages you may have to resort to sign language but often the children speak a little English.

Learning a few phrases of Greek will ensure your welcome. It is also worth remembering that the etiquette in the country is for the stranger to speak first, when meeting someone in the fields or when entering a shop or taverna.

FOOD

It is easy to eat out all over the island. In tavernas it is quite usual to walk into the kitchen to inspect the food and to choose your dish or piece of meat or fish and indicate how you would like it to be cooked. Fish is a very expensive dish throughout Crete, and is sold by weight. You choose your fish, they are weighed and then you order how they are to be cooked.

Only in the very touristy areas will you find restaurants as we understand them, but even in the most out of the way places you can obtain simple food in tavernas.

Greek salad is a good value classic snack for lunch. Tomatoes, olives, cucumbers, peppers and lettuce with white feta cheese. Bread is served automatically with all food.

Greek meals tend to come in batches not courses and it is quite usual to share, especially starters and salad and vegetable dishes. Main dishes are served with a garnish. If you order vegetables or chips they are regarded as a starter and will probably be served before the main dish.

For self catering and picnic shopping there are plenty of minimarkets in the tourist areas and villages and adjacent to the larger hotels. Interesting open markets can be found in Heraklion and Chania.

WEATHER

Winter lasts from November to March and this is the period of the highest rainfall. Rain does not however usually last long, although it falls as snow on the mountains and remains until late Spring. Despite this the climate on the coasts is still mild.

The weather can be very varied in Spring.

From March onwards the temperature rises, flowers enter the Spring flush and the weather begins to settle with temperatures in the 60s(17°C) and 70s(23°C) but there is always a chance of rain and wind, or even snow in the mountains, but these periods are usually short lived, even so it can be cool or even cold in the evenings in April and May, especially in accommodation designed for high summer.

Travel hint: Bring warm clothes and jackets as well as a sunhat and shorts if you visit in the Spring.

The south part of the island is always warmer than the north. By June, the temperature rises rapidly, and July and August are very hot indeed, although the sea breeze helps to ameliorate the effects of the heat.

In September the temperatures are still high and the first migrants are returning. October can have the first rains and temperatures start to fall. The winter months are cooler and wetter with always the chance of some good weather.

Wind is a constant feature of the island. If it blows from the north the it can hold up migrants and cause a 'fall' in the Spring. However if you find yourself in a windy spot where the area seems to have been swept clean of birds, then try crossing the island, you may find it surprisingly calm and offering shelter to local birds as well as migrants.

WHAT TO EXPECT DURING THE YEAR

AUTUMN-WINTER

November to March. The resident birds Stonechat, Chaffinch, Blue Rock Thrush, Bluetit, Great Tit, Goldfinch, Buzzard, Hooded Crow, Wren and Sardinian Warbler are joined by wintering Robins, Chiffchaff, Black Redstart and Mistle and Song Thrushes. Amongst the shore birds are the odd wintering Little Egret, while Mediterranean and Black-headed Gulls are common. Some Sandwich Terns winter and there can be one or two Kentish plovers along the shore. Ducks arrive to winter on the reservoirs and lakes as well as Black-necked Grebes. Some ducks may stay to bred. In 1993/94 there was an exceptional influx of Mute Swans. Most wintering passerines have left by the end of March and resident birds are beginning to breed by late March.

SPRING

March-May. The Swifts arrive in Chania about March 19th each year and are soon followed by the swallows. From then until mid-May there is a steady stream of arrivals of Summer migrants to join the resident breeding birds which have started nesting in March. Rüppell's Warbler's and Sub-alpine Warblers arrive in late March/early April while Orphean, Oliveaceous and Olivetree Warblers do not appear until May.

During April there is a steady stream of summer migrants passing through the island and Pied, Collared and Spotted Flycatchers can be common at certain periods. Whinchat, Woodchat Shrike, Rock Thrush, Little Bittern, Glossy Ibis, Little Egret as well as Purple, Grey and Great White Egret can pass through in waves, although they can pass overhead without stopping if the weather is clear and fine. Amongst the waders Little Stint are common, while Wood Sandpiper are frequent and Green and Common Sandpipers are seen, Redshank, Dunlin are less frequent and Black-winged Stilt, Avocet, Grey and Golden Plover pass through in small numbers. Little Ringed Plover arrive to breed, but Ringed and Kentish are passage migrants in small numbers. Occasionally there are rarer plovers or Flamingoes or Spoonbills but these are usually only seen after storms or days of heavy rain. Poor weather can bring good birding on Crete.

In the first few days of May Bee-eaters pass over in huge flocks streaming north to breed. They are more frequently heard than seen. They seem to use Aptera and Akrotiri near Chania as signposts.

SUMMER

June-August. This is the quiet period. The residents have finished breeding and the heat and dryness make birdwatching difficult but in the cooler mountains birds are still busy and in the gorges birds of prey can be seen although they too breed early in the year.

Kingfisher appear to depart from the island and are not seen again until Autumn.

On the offshore islands Eleanora's Falcons begin breeding.

LATE SUMMER-EARLY AUTUMN

August-October. The first migrants return either the unsuccessful breeders or successful offspring appear in early August onwards with a peak in late August/early September. Then throughout September and October migrants stream south. Some migrants such as Whitethroat and Red-backed Shrike are loop migrants and are only common in Autumn, usually in September.

Then the winter residents arrive and the cycle begins again with the passerines first and then the grebes and ducks appearing as the northern winter drives them south.

PLANTS OF CRETE

In Spring in March, April and May, the Cretan flora is at its best. The island offers a variety of zones from sea shore through maquis, mountain plateau to chasm where over 2,000 species of plants grow. Despite development there are interesting flowers everywhere. For the endemic hunter then the west and south are probably the best areas to visit. Crete is also famous for its orchids and the areas around archaeological sites are some of the best hunting grounds but any area such as the scrub hillside close to your hotel can be profitable.

The Mediterranean climate with mild wet winters and very hot dry summers has influenced the vegetation and many Cretan plants have adapted to withstand heat and drought and bloom after the rains in early Autumn, intermittently throughout the winter and especially in the Spring. Altitude affects the time of flowering as does the previous winter but the orchids usually begin in March with *Barlia robertiana*, being one of the first followed in April by the main flush with *Orchis papilionacae, O.coriophora, O.italica, O.simia, O.saccata, O.laxiflora, O.anatolica, O.quadripunctata*,and *Ophrys lutea, O.fusca, O.sphegodes, O.spruneri, O.fuciflora, O.scolopax, O.apifera, O.bombylifera, O. tenthredinifera*, and the tongue orchids, the Serapias, with *S.cordigera, vomaracea, lingua* and *parviflora*. Damp meadows can have drifts of *Anacamptis pyramidalis, Pyramid orchid*, and *O. laxiflora*.

Stony areas near the sea have *Anthemis rigida*, Yellow Horned Poppy *Glaucium flavum* and Sea Stock, *Matthiola sinuata*, with occasional vivid patches of the South African *Carpobrotus acinaciforme* - Hottentot Fig.

The waysides and fields have Crown Daisy *Chrysanthemum corinarium var. discolor*, Vipers Bugloss, Anchusa and houndstongues with poppies and Blue Pimpernel.

The hillside flora is formed by phygana and maquis. Maquis is a mixture of shrubs, subshrubs and small trees, mainly evergreen with an understorey of annuals, biennials and bulbs. Many are aromatic with reduced, felted or narrow leaves. Rock roses, *Cistus salvifolius, C.parvifolius*, and *C.incanus ssp creticus* mingle with Jerusalem Sage *Phlomis fruticosa*, Spanish broom and calicotome.

Phygana has low growing often prickly or felted plants with many aromatic herbs. In amongst this protection orchids such as *O.lutea, O.bombylifera* and *O.coriophora* grow and in the bare patches between are tiny irislike flowers which only flower for part of a day *Gynandriris sisyrinchium*. Cretan iris, *Iris unguicularis* grows from between rocks usually higher up in the mountains. On rock faces or out of walls in towns and monasteries wall lettuce *Petromarula pinnata* and *Verbascum arcturus* grow.

At the end of May these all die down until the Sea daffodils *Pancratium maritimum* and Sea squill *Urginea maritima* flower in late August from their seaside bulbs to herald the start of the Autumn bulb season.

ORCHID CHECKLIST

Aceras anththropophorum
Anacamptis pyramidalis
Barlia robertiana
Cephalanthera cucullata
C. damasonium
C. longifolia
Dactylorhiza romana
Epipactis cretica
E. microphylla
Himantoglossom caprinum
Limodorum abortivum subsp abortivum
Listera ovata
Neotinea maculata
Ophrys apifera
Ophrys basilissa
Ophrys bombyliflora
Ophrys candica sensu lato
Ophrys ciliata
Ophrys doerfleri (cretica)
Ophrys fleischmanni
Ophrys fusca
Ophrys heldreichii
Ophrys holoserica sensu lato
Ophrys holoserica subsp. holoserica
Ophrys holoserica subsp. maxima
Ophrys iricolor
Ophrys lutea subsp. lutea
Ophrys lutea subsp. minor
Ophrys mammosa
Ophrys omegaifera
Ophrys sitiaca
Ophrys sphegodes sensu lato
Ophrys sphegodes subsp. cretensis
Ophrys sphegodes subsp. gortynia
Ophrys spruneri
Ophrys tenthrendinifera

Orchis anatolica sensu lato
Orchis anatolica subsp. sitiaca
Orchis boryi
Orchis collina
Orchis coriophora subsp. fragrans
Orchis italica
Orchis lactea
Orchis laxiflora subsp. laxiflora
Orchis palustris
Orchis papilionacea
Orchis pauciflora
Orchis prisca
Orchis provincialis
Orchis quadripunctata
Orchis sancta
Orchis simia
Orchis tridentata
Serapias bergonii
Serapias cordigera
Serapias lingua
S. orientalis subsp. orientalis
Serapias parviflora
Spiranthes spiralis

BIRD SITES ON CRETE

A selection of the most interesting sites is listed below in alphabetical order. Numbers have also been allocated to each site listed and these numbers are marked on the sketch map of Crete.

Some sites are best visited at certain times of day and if this is important it is mentioned in the text, but in general the best time of day for birdwatching is from dawn to mid-morning, then on hot days the birds of prey use the thermals from 10.30am until about 2.00pm. During migration times, late afternoon can often produce another wave of diurnal migrants arriving to feed before moving off next morning.

This is probably still not a fully comprehensive site list for Crete but after some extensive reconnaisance of the island I believe that these are the most productive sites. However, as water is very scarce on Crete migrants and residents can be attracted to very small areas of water and so 'Anything can turn up anywhere.' Due to a continuous building programme along the coast many sites are disturbed or have suffered pollution from builders rubble. Do not let this put you off, the birds are often still using these areas.

BIRDS: Some indicaton of the range of birds is indicated. They are not listed in order but the most interesting migrants and vagrants are included.

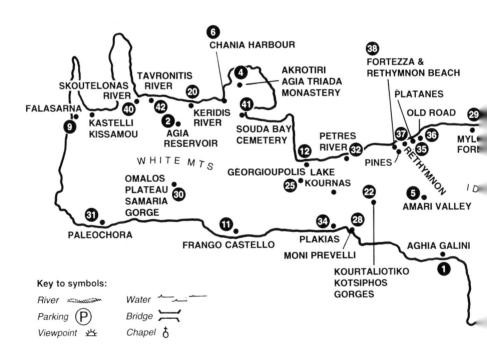

The common birds in Crete throughout the island are Chaffinch, Greenfinch, Goldfinch, Stonechat, Crested Lark, Sardinian Warbler, Cetti's Warbler, Great Tit, Italian Sparrow and Hooded Crow. These breed in the lowlands while in the uplands Bluetit, Wren and Blackbird are more common.

Passage waders and warblers are listed under the sites. They are mainly found in April. Migrants such as Hoopoe, Roller, Bee-eater, Olivaceous, Olivetree Warbler, Lesser Kestrel and Red-footed Falcon and Eleonora's Falcon usually return in late April early May, while Rüppell's Warbler, Bonelli's Warbler, and Cretzschmar's Bunting appear to return earlier in late March and early April. Some birds are more common as Spring migrants such as Pied Flycatcher and Woodchat Shrike, while Red-backed Shrikes and Lesser Whitethroats are loop migrants in the Autumn. Autumn migrants begin to return in August. Winter visitors have usually left by the end of March.

Birds of prey are common throughout the island with Buzzard and Kestrel everywhere. Griffon Vultures nest on every suitable cliff and in the gorges. Golden Eagles are thinly distributed, while Bonelli's Eagle, Booted Eagle and Lammergeier are found in quiet mountain gorges. The Lammergeier is fairly easy to see over Omalos or Lassithi plateaus occasionally associating with Griffon Vultures.

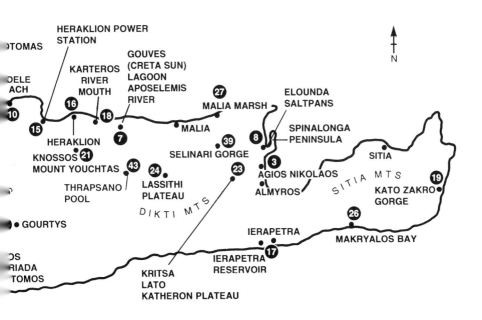

1. AGHIA GALINI and PLATIS RIVER.

LOCATION: On South coast, 62km south of Rethymnon, in the Gulf of Messara.

PARKING: At the edge of the village.

TIME OF YEAR: Spring   Summer   Autumn   Winter
                        *   /   *   ?

DESCRIPTION: Aghia Galini is a tourist village, its bay can hold flocks of Garganey in Spring. The Platis river runs to the east of the village. There is a path under the cliffs where Alpine Swifts nest. The river mouth has had herons, Great Snipe, Little Bittern, and picks up other migrants. There is a footbridge over the river and the surrounding scrub can also be good for migrants. The valley behind looks worthy of exploration.

BIRDS: Little Bittern, Purple Heron, Alpine Swift, Swift, Garganey, Great Reed Warbler, Little Ringed Plover, Wood Sandpiper, Marsh Sandpiper, Avocet, Great Snipe, Cetti's Warbler.

Map 1. AGHIA GALINI and PLATIS RIVER.

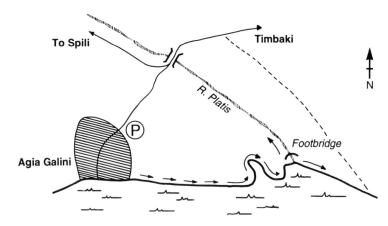

2. AYIA/AGIA RESERVOIR

LOCATION: Southwest of Chania en route to OMALOS.

PARKING: Early in the morning at the church in AYIA/AGIA. The village is now signed as you approach from Chania. The church is concealed behind a grove of Eucalyptus trees as you approach from Chania.

RESERVOIR: Take the track past the orangejuice factory down to the Great Spring pools of Ayia, which are now fenced and gated. Currently this is wired closed but can be opened. Please make sure you close the gate after you. If there is anyone about please ask permission to view by smiling and pointing at your binoculars, if you speak no Greek. Please do nothing to harm relations here in case the gate should be locked in the future.

DAM: Turn west in AYIA village past Taverna Restaurant 10 and right again in 500m after crossing over small bridge with metal railings. The track leads past orange groves to the dam.

TIME OF YEAR: Spring   Summer   Autumn   Winter
                        *   *   *   *

DESCRIPTION: The reservoir is a very good area for migrants and for breeding birds in the reeds. In the early morning the view from the dam is directly into the sun so the tracks near the church are better. The trees and scrub area nearby can also hold migrants. The reedbed area can be best seen from the dam.

BIRDS: Garganey, Little Crake, Spotted Crake, Marsh Harrier, Little Bittern, Night Heron, Squacco Heron, Whiskered Tern, Black Tern, White-winged Black Tern, Ruff, Wood Sandpiper, Greenshank, Willow Warbler, Spotted Flycatcher, Reed Warbler, Sedge Warbler, Moustached Warbler, Sand Martin, Red-rumped Swallow, Collared Pratincole, Yellow Wagtail.

Map 2. AYIA/AGIA RESERVOIR

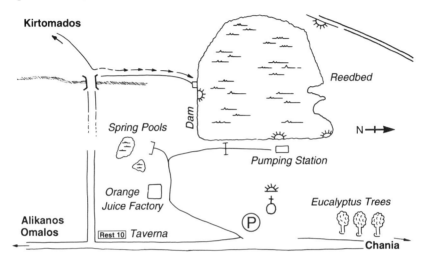

3. AGIOS NIKOLAOS - HARBOUR and ALMYROS MARSH.

LOCATION: AGIOS NIKOLAOS is 56 km east of Heraklion on the main coast road. The harbour is in the centre of town.
Almyros marsh is about 3km east along the Sitia road. It is possible to walk along the shore from the bus station to the marsh.

PARKING: Difficult in Agios Nikolaos.
For Almyros on seaward side at 2.5KM mark along Sitia road.

TIME OF YEAR: Spring   Summer   Autumn   Winter
                    *   /   *   *

DESCRIPTION: The town of Agios Nikolaos is very touristy, but the harbour is worth checking for Audouin's Gull, and Kingfishers which often perch on pipes in the harbour wall. Alpine Swifts nest in the cliffs below the Mirabello Hotel on the road out towards Elounda.

ALMYROS MARSH has a small reedbed and a spring which feeds it and the central small pool and then flows out into the bay. The small beach is disturbed so do visit early or late. For such a small area, it has produced a very good list.

BIRDS: Town: Audouin's Gull, Mediterranean Gull, Herring Gull, Kingfisher, Swift, Alpine Swift, Sardinian Warbler, Rüppells Warbler.
Almyros: Mediterranean Shearwater, Common Sandpiper, Common Tern, Little Tern, Wood Sandpiper, Avocet, Reed Warbler, Penduline Tit, Yellow Wagtail.

3. AGIOS NIKOLAOS - HARBOUR and ALMYROS MARSH.

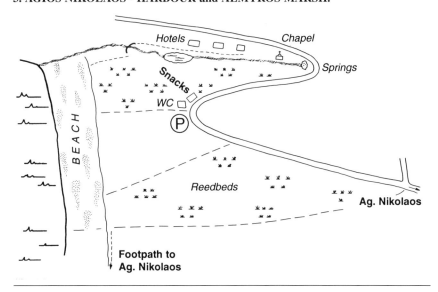

4.AKROTIRI PENINSULA and AGIA TRIADA MONASTERY.

LOCATION: AKROTIRI: The west coast has two small areas were there is freshwater.

VENEZELOS GRAVES: A park and memorial area with a viewpoint over Chania. Worth a stop if you are passing to check for migrants.

TERSANAS MARSH & POND: 2 Km NW of Horafakia on NW coast of Akrotiri, turn left towards TERSANAS village. The marsh can be seen below on the right. POND: Continue through the village, climb up to barren fields to a large pond, 100m from the last house of the village. P at roadside clearing.

There is also water at Kalotheroma on the road to Stavros between Kounoupidiana and Horafakia. Walk upstream on the dirt track beside the river.

MONASTERY: 17 km fron Chania. Follow the signs to the airport, and then to the monastery. The road is tarmaced as far as Agia Triada, but further rough roads lead on to the Moni Gouverneto Monastery. From this monastery it is possible to walk along cliff paths to a deserted monastery and hermit caves.

PARKING: At the monasteries.

TIME OF YEAR: Spring   Summer   Autumn   Winter
                    *   /   *   ?

DESCRIPTION: A promentory to the east of Chania which can be good for migrants. The scrub areas around and approaching the monastery and the new vineyard on the left of the avenue leading to the monastery usually attract migrants. The monastery courtyard has an interesting grafted citrus tree with four kinds of fruit. Scops Owls can roost in the garden. Between the two monasteries birds congregate to drink at sheep troughs, if they have been filled, as Akrotiri is dry. The garden at Moni Gouverneto can also hold migrants.

BIRDS: Pied Flycatcher, Hoopoe, Wheatear, Black-eared Wheatear, Scops Owl, Sparrowhawk, Chukar, Buzzard, Blue Rock Thrush, Chaffinch, Greenfinch, Tree Pipit, Collared Flycatcher, Wryneck, Whitethroat, Sardinian and Wood Warbler, Yellow Wagtail, Redstart, Ortolan, Swift.

Map 4. AKROTIRI PENINSULA and AGIA TRIADA MONASTERY.

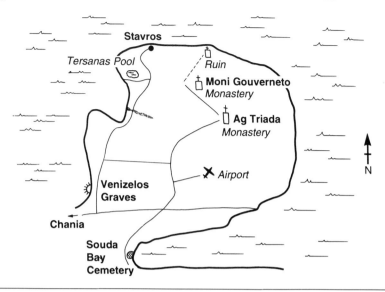

5. AMARI VALLEY

LOCATION: Southeast of Rethymnon. This upland valley offers a circular drive through a beautiful area with very attractive villages, and is very good for birds of prey. Travelling east from Rethymnon, turn off right, after 3km, crossing under the new bypass road.

PARKING: At lay-bys. With caution on the hill roads.

TIME OF YEAR: Spring   Summer   Autumn   Winter
                   *   *   *   ?

Map 5. AMARI VALLEY

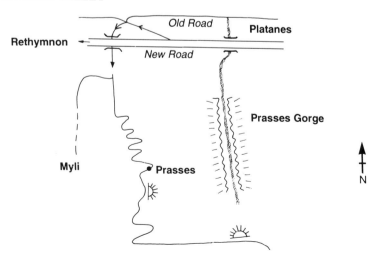

DESCRIPTION: This valley is a famous area for raptors. After climbing up into the mountains the road passes through the village of Prasses. Just as the view opens out there are views into a huge gorge to the east, where Griffon Vultures breed, and possibly Bonelli's Eagle. Park with care on the left roadside. Further on the east side of the valley and the hills behind Fourfouras are dominated by the Idha Mountains. This is reputed to be a fine area for raptors especially Short-toed Eagle.

The turn-off just at the start of the tour from Rethymnon signed to Khromonastiri leads in 4.5 km to Myli a deserted village where Lesser Kestrel used to breed in the cliffs above the old village.

BIRDS: Griffon Vultures, Kestrel, Lesser Kestrel, Lanner, Short-toed Eagle, Buzzard, Peregrine, Stonechat, Woodchat Shrike, Booted Eagle, Bonelli's Eagle, Sardinian Warbler, Chaffinch, Cirl Bunting.

6. CHANIA HARBOUR

LOCATION: At the east end of the town.

PARKING: Difficult in Chania. There are no car parks, just street parking and some meter parking in the centre. It is possible to park near the west and eastern ends of the harbour with a little map reading.

TIME OF YEAR: Spring   Summer   Autumn   Winter
                   *   /   *   ?

DESCRIPTION: An attractive town clustered round a pedestrianised harbour. There is a gull and heron roost at the edge of the harbour. The best views are from the small park in the ramparts to the east of the Porto Veneziano Hotel. Early morning observations are difficult because of the direction of the sun unless you are there before sunrise. In the evening the roost begins to gather from 6.30pm onwards. Chania is full of Swifts, and interesting gulls and terns can drift into the harbour. There are now artifical rocks off the mouth of the harbour which also attracts a roost as well the rocks off the east end of the harbour.The tamarisks around the swimming pool west of the harbour are worth checking in the Autumn.

BIRDS: Little Egret, Grey Heron, Mediterranean Gull, Yellow-legged Gull, Little Tern, Sandwich Tern, Common Tern, Common Sandpiper, Swift, Alpine Swift. Autumn: Olivaceous Warbler, Icterine Warbler, Wood Warbler, Willow Warbler, Chiffchaff, Barred Warbler, Kingfisher.

Map 6. CHANIA HARBOUR

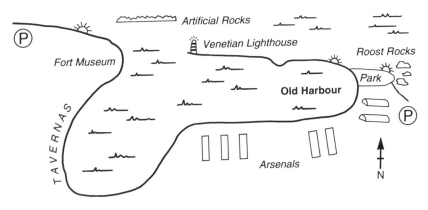

7. GOUVES (CRETA SUN) LAGOON and APOSELEMIS RIVER

LOCATION: On north coast 21km east of Heraklion between KM157 and KM156.
For the lagoon turn off at sign to Creta Sun Hotel.
For the river continue along the main road for another km.

PARKING: For Gouves Lagoon, at hotel laundry which is the last building on left before hotel gates.
For Aposelemis River, on main road on seawardside, at advertising sign at bridge with between KM157 and KM156.

TIME OF YEAR: Spring   Summer   Autumn   Winter
                 *   /   *   *

DESCRIPTION: The Aposelemis river runs from the bridge. There is much rubbish and builder's rubble and the water level can be very low but many migrants and breeding birds are attracted to this area.
The Gouves (Creta Sun)lagoon is formed by the shore shingle damming the river as it enters the sea. This lagoon picks up a good variety of waders and interesting vagrants, and it is usually dry by the end of May. Current species list is 147+.

DIRECTIONS: For APOSELEMIS RIVER walk down the west side of the river towards the sea. After the last building on your left turn west and then south again keeping a large tree on the right. Continue on down to the shore and river mouth pools.

BIRDS: Cory's Shearwater, Purple Heron, Griffon Vulture, Buzzard, Booted Eagle, Honey Buzzard, Snipe, Great Snipe, Whimbrel, Gull-billed Tern, Caspian Tern, Glossy Ibis, Little Ringed Plover, Ringed Plover, Ruff, Reed Warbler, Sedge Warbler, Garganey, Ferruginous Duck, Teal, Pintail, Tufted Duck, Red-rumped Swallow, Flamingo, Marsh Sandpiper, Wood Sandpiper, Kentish Plover, Temminck's and Little Stint, Grey Plover, White-tailed Plover, Sociable Plover, Whinchat, Stonechat, Sardinian Warbler, Bonelli's

---

Map 7. GOUVES (CRETA SUN) LAGOON and APOSELEMIS RIVER

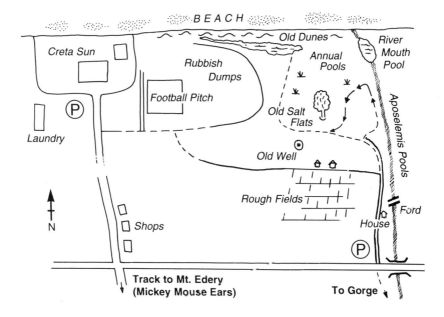

Warbler, Spotted Flycatcher, Calandra Lark, Red-throated Pipit, Yellow Wagtail, Fan-tailed Warbler, Garden Warbler, Collared Flycatcher, Woodchat Shrike, Starling, Corn Bunting, Wryneck, Short-toed Lark.

8. ELOUNDA SALTPANS and SPINALONGA PENINSULA.

LOCATION: 10 Km North of Agios Nikolaos. Turn off the new road at the edge of Agios Nikolaos. Elounda can also be reached from Neapolis. Turn off onto the old road at Neapolis and follow signs. Just off this route there is an interesting pool near Limnes and the area is a good for Kestrel, Lanner and other birds of prey.

PARKING: In Square at Elounda.

TIME OF YEAR: Spring   Summer   Autumn   Winter
                  *   /   *   *

DESCRIPTION: Elounda saltpans lie between the village and Spinalonga Peninsula. The old saltpans are reached from the village by walking towards Agios Nikolaos and turning left at the disco towards Spinalonga. Walk round the back of the pans to check on the dry areas. Then continue on around the path at the back of the pans and follow the wall and track back to the road across to the peninsula. The rough fields to the right before crossing the bridge, are worth checking for pipits, wagtails, buntings, wheatears and even quail. If arriving by foot or bus, walk to the old saltpans from the main road on the tracks at the Palm tree, opposite the Taverna Avenita. Spinalonga peninsula can have interesting breeding birds and migrants if they are moving through. The tracks on the peninsula lead through to small fields and rocky bays.
Elounda could be a good centre. Donkey tracks along Cape Ag. Ioannis, and up to the windmills above Plaka, which is a good watching point, lead into good country for migrants and eagles. PLAKA bay is also a migrant roost area for herons and ducks.
The valleys behind Elounda to the west and north are also interesting. The track up to the Elounda rubbish tip leads up to a pass and a hidden valley where raptors and migrants pass through and drink at the wells.

BIRDS: Saltpans: Night Heron, Squacco Heron, Little Bittern, Black-winged Stilt, Wood Sandpiper, Green Sandpiper, Common Sandpiper, Little Stint, Temminck's Stint, Ruff,

---

Map 8. ELOUNDA SALTPANS and SPINALONGA PENINSULA.

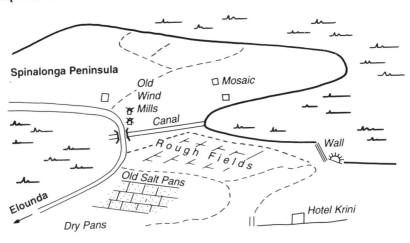

20

Curlew Sandpiper, Little Ringed Plover, Ringed Plover, Kentish Plover, Cirl Bunting, Quail, Red-throated Pipit, Crested Lark, Short-toed Lark, Tawny Pipit, Black Tern, White-winged Black Tern, Whiskered Tern, Yellow Wagtails, Ortolan and Corn Bunting.
Hillsides: Goshawk, Raven, Hooded Crow, Griffon Vulture, Golden Eagle, Kestrel, Peregrine, Hobby, Golden Oriole.

9. FALASARNA

LOCATION: On west coast, west of Kastelli Kissamou. Turn off right just after passing a petrol station near Platanos. This road is unmarked. If you miss it take the next right (signed) at the edge of Platanos. At the T junction in view of the sea turn right.

PARKING: At tavernas at end of tarmaced road, or at the archaeological site further along on the rough track.

TIME OF YEAR: Spring   Summer   Autumn   Winter
                    *   /   *   ?

DESCRIPTION: There are four main areas worth checking for birds. Firstly below the tavernas to the south is a rough area of scrub. Then to the north of the tavernas along the beach is a pool where waders and herons can feed. Migrants can be observed following the coast north and out to sea amongst the small islands there is the possibility of Shags, Eleonora's Falcons, shearwaters and gulls. Away from the shore the track through the olive groves and plastic greenhouse fields leading to the archaeological site can hold flycatchers, warblers, shrikes, wheatears and larks. The ridge of the hillside above is very good for raptors and ravens. Finally the shore scrub around the archaeological site and the Hellenistic harbour has breeding Black-eared Wheatear, Subalpine Warbler, Sardinian Warbler.

Map 9. FALASARNA

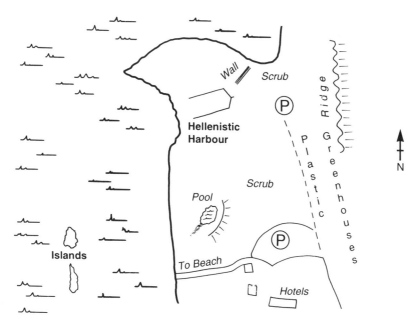

21

BIRDS: Shag, Little Egret, Grey Heron, Griffon Vulture, Lammergeier, Buzzard, Sparrowhawk, Goshawk, Eleonora's Falcon, Kestrel, Common Sandpiper, Alpine Swift, Rock Dove, Crested Lark, Woodlark, Short-toed Lark, House and Sand Martin, Raven, Great Tit, Blue Tit, Blue Rock Thrush, Black-eared Wheatear, Whinchat, Nightingale, Cetti's Warbler, Great Reed Warbler, Pied Flycatcher, Woodchat Shrike, Black-headed Bunting, Garden Warbler, Whitethroat, Blackcap.
Autumn: Golden Eagle, Bonelli's Eagle, Red Kite, Red-backed Shrike, Spanish Sparrow, Eleanora's Falcon.

10. FODELE RIVER and BEACH.

LOCATION: On the main coast road, west of Heraklion, between KM 117 and KM 116.

PARKING: In large lay-by after Petrol station on seaward side for beach and fields. Or at roadside after the turnoff to Fodele for RIVER.

TIME OF YEAR: Spring   Summer   Autumn   Winter
                   *   /   *   ?

DESCRIPTION: The stream runs alongside the side road to Fodele and down to the beach. The fields are on the land side of the main road, just across from the lay-by car park can hold migrants. Both these areas are worth checking for shrikes and other migrants. It is only possible to park when travelling west. Turn off towards Fodele to park when travelling east. The whole area is now overlooked by the Fodele Beach Hotel complex and it may no longer be a productive spot.
BIRDS: Cetti's Warbler, Sardinian Warbler, Orphean Warbler, Blackcap, Woodchat Shrike, Masked Shrike, Yellow Wagtails.

11. FRANGOCASTELLO

LOCATION: On the south coast 12 km east of Chora Sfakion. It can also be reached from Plakias, but a section of this road is still not surfaced and it is a hard drive, although the scenery is wonderful.

PARKING: At the castle and taverna.

Map 11. FRANGOCASTELLO

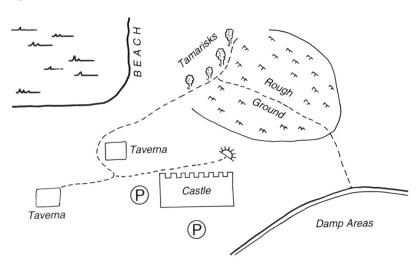

TIME OF YEAR: Spring   Summer   Autumn   Winter
                     *   /   *   ?

DESCRIPTION: There is an area of rough and sometimes marshy ground to the north of the castle, which can be good for herons, Glossy Ibis and pratincoles. The best area for migrants is in the scrub west of the castle and the beach can be good for waders early and late in the day.

BIRDS: Little Stint, Wood Sandpiper, Common Sandpiper, Collared Pratincole, Grey Heron, Little Egret, Glossy Ibis, Black-eared Wheatear, Wryneck, Pied Flycatcher, Collared Flycatcher.

12. GEORGIOUPOLIS LAKE

LOCATION: On the north coast halfway between Rethymnon and Chania.
From RETHYMNON: Turn off heading west between KM 37 and KM 36. Take the first left in the square, the lake is down a Eucalyptus avenue.
From CHANIA: turn off heading east after the EKO petrol station at KM 30 and continue on the old road for 4 km.

PARKING: On Georgioupolis side of the new bridge over the old road.

TIME OF YEAR: Spring   Summer   Autumn   Winter
                     *   *   *   *

DESCRIPTION: The lake is fed by fresh water springs and the River Almyros. The best view point is from the roadside on the Georgioupolis side of the bridge.
The area to the east of the village has reedbeds and more springs. This area is being encroached on by houses and hotels.
The rivermouth, the beach, harbour and Eucalyptus avenue are all worth checking in the Spring and Autumn.

BIRDS: Little Bittern, Bittern, Little Egret, Purple Heron, Booted Eagle, Marsh Harrier, Little Crake, Spotted Crake, Black Tern, White-winged Black Tern, Little Grebe, Moorhen, Coot, Nightingale, Cuckoo, Scops Owl, Reed Warbler, Cetti's Warbler, Golden Oriole, Woodchat Shrike, Swallow, Sand Martin, Yellow Wagtail, White Wagtail, Kingfisher.

13. GEROPOTAMOS BRIDGE

LOCATION: On main road west of Heraklion between KM 75 and KM 74.

PARKING: Parking only on seaward side of the road, west of the bridge.

TIME OF YEAR: Spring   Summer   Autumn   Winter
                     *   /   *   ?

DESCRIPTION: A pool at the river mouth. The bridge allows a good view point over the pool. This can be good if migrants are moving or it may be empty depending on your luck. To walk down to the river cross the road to the south side and follow a broad track away from the river in 50+ metres turn left down a concrete track down to the river and under the bridge to the beach and pool. There are also tracks up stream.

BIRDS: Common Sandpiper, Little Ringed Plover, Little Tern, White-winged Black Tern, Willow Warbler, Swallow, House Martin, Red-rumped Swallow, Tawny Pipit, Wheatear, Yellow Wagtail.

14. GOURTYS

LOCATION: An archaeological site 44 km south of Heraklion, with a stream, hillside and olive groves en route to PHAESTOS and AGHIA TRIADA.

PARKING: At archaeological site

TIME OF YEAR: Spring   Summer   Autumn   Winter
                *   ?   /   ?

DESCRIPTION: Archaeological site with dry hillside and olive groves. A stream flowing at the south side of the site attracts migrants and breeding warblers.
From the carpark walk south across the bridge on the main road and turn right and follow track alongside the stream. The hillside above with the Acropolis on top is frequented by birds of prey. The olive groves can be interesting behind the site and to the east of the main road. Walk north along the road and then follow the site signs. This is best early before the first coach parties arrive if possible.

BIRDS: Kestrel, Lesser Kestrel, Golden Eagle, Buzzard, Blackcap, Sardinian Warbler, Woodchat Shrike, Goldfinch, Willow Warbler, Pied Flycatcher, Spotted Flycatcher,

Map 14. GOURTYS

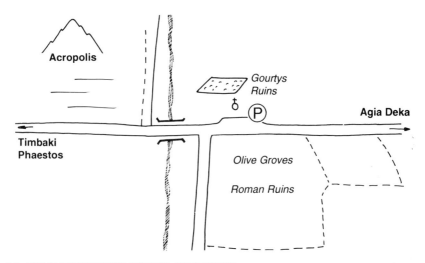

15. HERAKLION POWER STATION

LOCATION: 5km west of the town on the old coast road. Travelling west from Heraklion exit at Chania Gate and turn off following signs to Akti Zeus Hotel. Travelling east or west on the new road turn off at the Power station.

PARKING: Roadside parking or at the River Center.

TIME OF YEAR: Spring   Summer   Autumn   Winter
                *   /   *   *

DESCRIPTION: An area of rough land between the Akti Zeus Hotel and the Power station, and east of the Hotel towards the Agapi Beach Hotel there are rough shore fields. A river curves round behind and across the site towards the sea. There is a gull roost offshore at the Power Station. The Station is being enlarged and development is continuing apace. The area is disturbed during the day, but waders continue to feed on insects in the floating weed on the river. Herons use the pools scattered throughout the area.

BIRDS: Mediterranean Gull, Herring Gull, Lesser Black-backed Gull, Sardinian Warbler, Woodchat Shrike, Yellow Wagtail, Ruff, Little Stint, Fan-tailed Warbler, Hoopoe, Marsh Harrier, Wood Sandpiper.

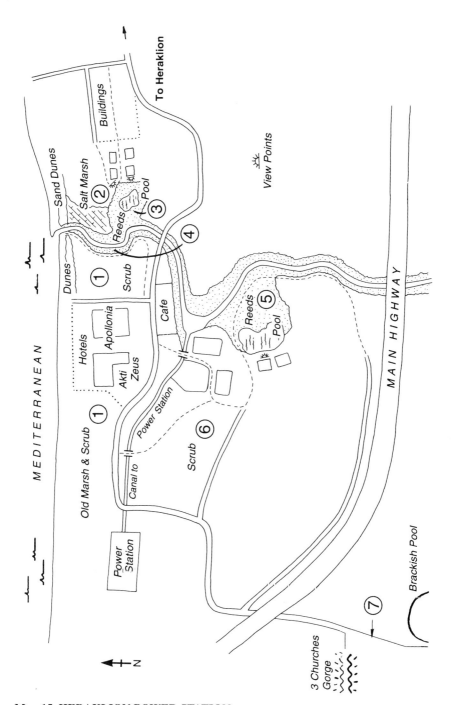

Map 15. HERAKLION POWER STATION

25

16. HERAKLION TOWN and HARBOUR

LOCATION: The harbour is well signposted.

PARKING: In harbour area.

TIME OF YEAR: Spring   Summer   Autumn   Winter
                  *   /·   *   *

DESCRIPTION: The harbour can hold a gull roost which has attracted interesting gull species included Audouin's and Great Black-headed. Over the town Swifts are common. House Sparrows and Italian Sparrows are both found. Dia island offshore has breeding Eleonora's Falcons.

BIRDS: Swift, Pallid Swift, House Sparrow, Italian Sparrow, Mediterranean Gull, Little Gull, Audouin's Gull, Great Black-headed Gull, Eleonora's Falcon.

17. IERAPETRA HARBOUR AND BRAMIANOS RESERVOIR.

LOCATION: Ierapetra lies on the south coast 38 km from Agios Nikolaos. The reservoir is situated on the west side of Ierapetra. Follow the main road west and at the edge of Ierapetra turn right signposted to Bramianos. It can also be reached from the north coast via Kalamavka.

PARKING: On the sea front for the harbour.

RESERVOIR: After the dam take the second road right. It is possible to drive and use the car as a hide, but the east side is still very raw and most of the birds are on the west side.

TIME OF YEAR: Spring   Summer   Autumn   Winter
                  *   /   *   *

DESCRIPTION: Ierapetra seafront can pick up terns and gulls.
The reservoir is developing nicely, and there is already a gull roost. Waders, herons and terns are passage migrants. Increasing numbers of ducks winter.

BIRDS: Little Egret, Glossy Ibis, Garganey, Wood Sandpiper, Common Sandpiper, Black Tern, Herring Gull, Mediterranean Gull, Black-headed Gull, Crested Lark, Tawny Pipit, Little Stint, Wigeon, Gadwall, Teal, Mallard, Pintail, Garganey, Shoveler, Pochard, Ferruginous Duck, Tufted Duck.

18. KARTEROS RIVER MOUTH

LOCATION: 8 Km east of HERAKLION on old coast road. From Heraklion town follow signs to airport, turn right just before the airport signed to Aghios Nikolaos to follow the old coast road. After 8 km there is a small church built into the rock, on a bend on the right. The marshy area begins on the left from this corner. the river runs between two football pitches. From the Heraklion by-pass follow signs to Karteros. At T junction turn left, for the church. Best visited morning or evening.

PARKING: At roadside for the stream at Amnissos.
On side road in Karteros, turn opposite Taverna Kavouri and park at the blue gates.

TIME OF YEAR: Spring   Summer   Autumn   Winter
                  *   /   *   *

DESCRIPTION: A river mouth just past the chapel at Amnissos and a small rough area/marsh between Karteros and the sea. The marshy area is best approached from Karteros. It is also possible to walk down the river to the sea, starting at a track by an Agave plant (large cactus) just before the turn off for Prases.

BIRDS: Little Egret, Garganey, Yellow Wagtails, Short-toed Larks, Marsh Harrier, Great Reed Warbler, Common, Wood & Marsh Sandpiper, Black-winged Stilt, Little Stint, Night, Squacco & Purple Heron.

Map 18. KARTEROS RIVER MOUTH

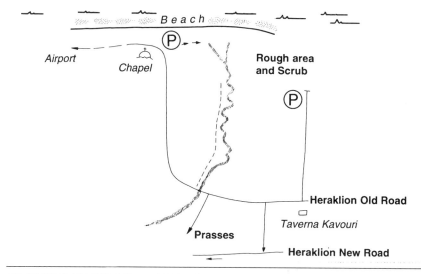

19. KATO ZAKROS and KATO ZAKROS GORGE.

LOCATION: 46 km southeast of Sitia.

PARKING: To walk through the gorge park at a lay-by before a sharp right hand bend 2 km out of Ano Zakros village. Park at the beach at Kato Zakro for archaeological site and marshy area, 5 km further on.

TIME OF YEAR: Spring   Summer   Autumn   Winter
               *   /   *   *

DESCRIPTION: The gorge leads down to the Valley of the Dead. The path is the middle of three which heads downhill into the gorge. It starts as a wide track but narrows and becomes rough and follows the river bed through to Kato Zakro. It is possible to catch a bus back to the car. The walk takes at least an hour without stops. It is very good for butterflies as well as flowers and birds. The valley can have nesting Blue Rock Thrush, Griffon Vultures, Ravens, Peregrine, and Kestrels.

At Kato Zakro the springs emerge within the archaeological site. Here Little Egrets, Squacco Herons, and Wood Sandpipers feed amongst the ruins. Continue past the site to walk up the gorge. This is a dry river bed and the actual path alters every year.

The river mouth area is surrounded by rushes and is worth checking.

BIRDS: Blue Rock Thrush, Peregrine, Griffon Vulture, Little Crake, Little Egret, Grey Heron, Eleonora's Falcon, Kestrel, Lesser Kestrel, Little Bittern, Squacco Heron, Crag Martin, Wood Sandpiper, Cuckoo, Whinchat, Black-eared Wheatear, Turtle Dove, Woodchat Shrike, Rock Dove, Scops Owl, Crested Lark, Golden Oriole, Pied Flycatcher.

20. KERIDIS RIVER MOUTH AND BEACH.

LOCATION: Thirteen km west of Chania. At KM 13 sign the main road crosses the river on a large bridge. Signed GERANI on the west bank and PLATANIAS on the east bank.

PARKING: 50m west from the bridge, or turn off directly after crossing the travelling west in front of a sign to Venus Pool Bar, into a field.

DESCRIPTION: A large river with sandbanks which can be viewed from the bridge. Both banks of the river are clothed in Giant reed *Arundo donax* which can hide herons or feeding flycatchers and warblers. Tracks lead from the carpark area , through an area of rough scrub to the sea. The beach area and the mouth of the river and the scrub area to the west and east are all interesting areas during migration times.

BIRDS: Black Kite, Grey Heron, Little Bittern, Fan-tailed Warbler, Stonechat, Whinchat, Tree Sparrow, Cirl Bunting, Pied Flycatcher, Cetti's Warbler, Common Sandpiper, Cormorant, Cory's Shearwater, Manx Shearwater, Stone Curlew, Eleonora's Falcon, Great Snipe, Wheatear, Kentish Plover, Chiff-chaff.

21. KNOSSOS VALLEY AND MOUNT YOUCHTAS.

LOCATION: From HERAKLION exit via Dimokratias Ave off Liberty Sq. If you are using the by pass, turn off at the traffic lights and follow the KNOSSOS signs. Continue on through Archanes to MOUNT YOUCHTAS.
Drive through Archanes, after about 3km, there is a right turn signed Giouhtas. Turn west here and immediately take the right fork, up the mountain track. (This is claimed to be possible in a Fiat Panda). After many turns you reach a saddle between the two peaks and a small pine wood with a wire fence on the left. Park on the left and walk on a track through the gap in the fence. After about 100 metres you came to a cliff edge with a fantastic view. There should be views of Griffon Vultures cruising by.

PARKING: KNOSSOS-At archaeological site, or down on a lane to Makrytikos on left immediately before the site. Entrance is free on Sundays and the area is very busy. There are charges for parking in some places, apply caution.
MT YOUCHTAS - At roadside at turn off or on track for Mt. Youchtas.

TIME OF YEAR: Spring   Summer   Autumn   Winter
                    *   ?   *   ?

DESCRIPTION: The valley attracts migrants and raptors. The hillside pines at the edge of the archaeological site are worth checking for warblers and serins. The hillside to the east after crossing the stream is good for orchids and raptor watching. To reach the hillside take the lane to Makrytikos, you may have to wade the ford before climbing up onto the flower covered slopes. Jackdaws nest in the Morisini viaduct.
MOUNT YOUCHTAS has breeding Kestrels, Griffon Vultures and offers good views over Heraklion. Alongside the track many orchids grow particularly on the lower section.

BIRDS: Knossos: Kestrel, Buzzard, Harriers, Serin, Golden Oriole, Red-rumped Swallow, Jackdaw colony, Scops Owl.
Youchtas: Griffon Vulture, Kestrel, Peregrine, Blue Rock Thrush, Subalpine Warbler, Sardinian Warbler, Whitethroat, Crag Martin.

22. KOURTALIOTIKO GORGE and KOTSIPHOS GORGE.

LOCATION: KOURTALIOTIKO GORGE is south of Rethymnon en route to PLAKIAS. The KOTSIPHOS is reached by following the signs to Selia and Frangocastelli before reaching the KOURTALIOTIKO. It is possible to drive a circular tour of both gorges. From PLAKIAS it is possible to walk up to the KOTSIPHOS GORGE, via the olive groves to the old mill and then take the broad track on the west to the gorge.

PARKING: At a large lay-by in the KOURTALIOTIKO.
With caution in the KOTSIPHOS.

TIME OF YEAR: Spring   Summer   Autumn   Winter
                    *   ?   ?   ?

DESCRIPTION: A good viewpoint for raptors particularly Griffon Vultures, Lammergeier, and Golden Eagle. The Megalopotamos flows through the Kourtaliotiko Gorge and emerges in the MONI PREVELLI valley. There are two chapels in the gorge. One is down a long flight of steps and one above the road. These offer some access to the gorge other than the road.

The KOTSIPHOS is an important route for raptors particularly Golden Eagle through the mountains from the south to the north in Spring.

BIRDS: Lammergeier, Griffon Vulture, Golden Eagle, Rock Dove, Crag Martin, Hobby, Peregrine, Swift, Alpine Swift, Blue Rock Thrush, Wren, Rüppell's Warbler, Blue Tit, White Wagtail, Chough, Jackdaw.

Map 22. KOURTALIOTIKO GORGE and KOTSIPHOS GORGE.

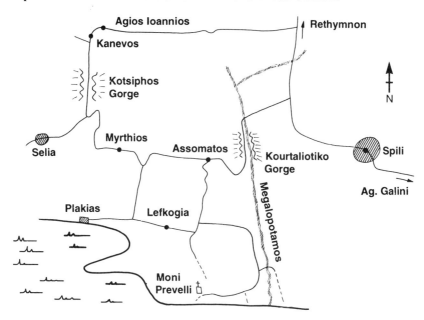

23. KRITSA, LATO, and KATHARON PLATEAU.

LOCATION: 8 km south from Agios Nikolaos.

PARKING: At church at Panagia Kera, for Lato, and outside Kritsa on right at the beginning of the one way system.
Park anywhere with care on Katharon Plateau.

TIME OF YEAR: Spring   Summer   Autumn   Winter
                    *   ?   /

DESCRIPTION: Kritsa is a village devoted to the sale of local handicrafts. The road up to it is good for raptors, it continues through Kritsa where it is very narrow, and then climbs 16 km up to the less well known KATHARON PLATEAU, which is very good for birds of prey, wheatears and flowers in Spring and Autumn. The road is rough; it is being improved but it is still hard on a hire car, 4 wheeled drive would be better, or a motorbike

29

with care.
From outside Kritsa a road leads off to LATO a fine Doric settlement in a pass. This road is now surfaced but the area can be interesting for warblers, cuckoos, wheatears, peregrines and hobbys.

BIRDS: Long-legged Buzzard, Buzzard, Golden Eagle, Peregrine, Hobby, Griffon Vulture, Egyptian Vulture, Lesser Kestrel, Rüppell's Warbler, Sardinian Warbler, Eleonora's Falcon, Blue Rock Thrush, Cuckoo, Wheatear, Black-eared Wheatear, Chiffchaff, Willow Warbler.

24. LASSITHI PLATEAU

LOCATION: About 60 km east from Heraklion, or it can be reached from Neapolis, or from Stalis to Moxos via a recently improved road with impressive views. From Agios Nikolaos take the old Heraklion road and turn left where it runs under the new road 5 km from Agios Nikolaos.

PARKING: Lay-bys and at the Psychro Cave.

TIME OF YEAR: Spring   Summer   Autumn   Winter
                 *   ?   *   /

DESCRIPTION: A fine mountain drive usually with good birds of prey especially when the thermals start after 10.00am. A very old plane tree in the village of Krasi, is worth the minor detour and may even have migrants in its ancient branches. The Seli Ambelou Pass into the plateau is a fine raptor watching area. There is a taverna below the windmills on the pass. The plateau is flat and fertile and has Quail, Cirl Bunting, Stonechat, Black-eared Wheatear. There are many tracks across the plateau and the damp areas can attract duck and waders. This is best approached by taking the anti-clockwise circuit round the plateau. The clockwise route, the usual way to the PSYCHRO CAVE (entrance fee) is a good watching point for Griffon Vultures, Chough, and Lammergeier, and Crag Martins breed in the cave. The eastern approach through Mesa Potami is excellent for Golden Eagles, as is the road from Stalis - Mohos - Omalos.

Map 24. LASSITHI PLATEAU

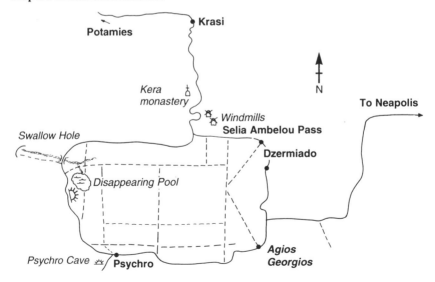

BIRDS: Griffon Vulture, Black-eared Wheatear, Wheatear, Chough, Crag Martin, Corn Bunting, Lammergeier, Buzzard, Kestrel, Peregrine, Golden Eagle, Blue Thrush, Cirl Bunting, Bluetit, Yellow Wagtails, Ortolan and Cretzschmar's Bunt. Stonechat, Chaffinch, Crested Lark, House Martin.

25. LAKE KOURNAS.

LOCATION: North of GEORGIOUPOLIS. Lake Kournas is signposted from the village.

PARKING: At the taverna.

TIME OF YEAR:	Spring	Summer	Autumn	Winter
	*	?	*	*

DESCRIPTION: A curiously clear blue lake. with tracks to the dam on the N side, and also on the south side past the tavernas. The area is best in late autumn/winter/early spring. The area is famous for Black-necked Grebe and duck. Other interesting good birds can turn up on the water and in the surrounding scrub. There is disturbance from pedalos so visit early and avoid Sundays, despite all this the birdlist is over 90.

BIRDS: Black-necked Grebe, Little Grebe, Ferruginous Duck, Pintail, Garganey, Coot. Coal Tit, Olivaceous Warbler, Buzzard, Common Sandpiper, Turtle Dove.

26. MAKRYALOS BAY and RIVER POOL.

LOCATION: On the South coast east of Ierapetra. The bay is a good watching point for migrants. The river is east of Makryalos itself. Shortly after leaving the village, take the first right on to the old coast road, 300m to 400m further on is a concrete bridge with hand rails.

PARKING: On old road.

TIME OF YEAR:	Spring	Summer	Autumn	Winter
	*	/	?	?

DESCRIPTION: The river from Azali/Lihines forms a pool which can hold migrants. Makryalos Bay is a very good bay for spring migrants.

BIRDS: Cory's Shearwater, Grey Heron, Purple Heron, Little Egret, Crane, Garganey, Glossy Ibis, Wood Sandpiper, Little Ringed Plover, Hoopoe, Red-rumped Swallow, Subalpine Warbler, Cetti's Warbler, Yellow Wagtail.

27. MALIA MARSH.

LOCATION: On north coast east of Heraklion. 2 km east of the town of Malia. Turn off to the sea travelling east between KM 173 and KM 174 at the turning point signposted Malia Antiquities.

PARKING: At Minoan site car park. If you are short of time or need to get a car close turn off in the centre of Malia, signed BEACH. Take the first right and drive down to the Malia Bay Hotel to Park.

TIME OF YEAR:	Spring	Summer	Autumn	Winter
	*	/	*	?

DESCRIPTION: This is an area of rough and cultivated fields and a rapidly diminishing marsh, with a recently tarmaced road between it and the beach. A small stream flows through the marshy area and has an outlet to the sea across the beach. Do not be put off by the draining and encroachment, it is still a very productive area.

DIRECTIONS: Walk west towards the sea from the car park. Once past the edge of the archaeological excavations, the fields on either side of the track can be productive eg.Tree Pipit, Tawny Pipit, Red-throated Pipit, Yellow Wagtails. Turn towards the sea and then walk east. This area of cultivated fields and scrub, which is also the area where the famous bee pendant was excavated usually has Stone Curlew, Hoopoe, Short-toed Lark, Wheatear, Whinchat, and Collared Pratincole in Spring.

Return by walking along the shallow shore cliffs towards Malia. In rough weather there can be Manx and Cory's Shearwaters in the bay. Early in the morning the beach can be good for waders and herons.

MALIA MARSH: East: Can be overlooked from the rough field next to the taverna (expensive) and walk along the path to the concrete bridge. The centre of this area is no longer worth exploring. West: Another overview point is from the old sand dunes near the Malia Bay Hotel.

BIRDS: Marsh Harrier, Red-footed Falcon, Grey and Purple Heron, Little Egret, Garganey, Wood Sandpiper, Collared Pratincole, Stone Curlew, Red-throated Pipit, Tawny Pipit, Red-backed Shrike, Woodchat Shrike, Lesser Grey Shrike, Yellow Wagtail, Hirundines, Short-toed Lark, Crested Lark, Woodchat Shrike, Cetti's Warbler, Fan-tailed Warbler, Reed Warbler, Kingfisher, Kestrel, Cirl Bunting.

28. MONI PREVELLI AND MEGALOPOTAMOS VALLEY.

LOCATION: On the south coast. 35 km south from Rethymnon and 8 km east of Plakias. Turn off on a tarmaced road just north of Lefkogia.

PARKING: At bridge over Megalopotamos.
At both the old and new monasteries.

TIME OF YEAR: Spring   Summer   Autumn   Winter
                    *   ?   *   ?

DESCRIPTION: The valley has a huge cliff which can be seen from the old Turkish bridge. Griffon Vultures nest and can be seen by late morning often stacking in the thermals. The old monastery area is often good for migrant warblers as are the banks of the river south from the bridge. Three km further on is the Moni Prevelli monastery which has a fine view over the Libyan Sea. Unfortunately in 1985 a fire burnt the lovely hillside below the monastery, but some scrub and pines do remain. Walk 50m. back from the car park and follow the track downhill towards the remaining pines. Further down the hill is a monks cell and chapel with a spring. Below here is a good area for Rüppell's Warblers. A track also leads down to the MEGALOPOTAMOS. This is about 1 km back along the road from the Monastery. A broad dirt track with parking, leads across and then down a cliff path to the river mouth. The valley is full of the endemic palm *Phoenix theophrastii.* In Spring it is also full of nudists! The river area has Grey Wagtail, Rock Dove, and Peregrine.

BIRDS: Little Egret, Griffon Vulture, Peregrine, Black-eared Wheatear, Cirl Bunting, Cretzschmar's Bunting, Turtle Dove, Rock Dove, Cuckoo, Golden Oriole, Ortolan, Rüppells Warbler, Blue Rock Thrush, Nightingale, Redstart, Wood Warbler, Tree Pipit, Spotted Flycatcher.

29. MYLO RIVER.

LOCATION: 20 Km east of Rethymnon. Take new road from Rethymnon and turn off at signs to Perama, about 1 Km along this road there is a track to the right leading to the Mylo river and a ford which is now dry. A few kilometres further along the road when Perama is in sight the river can be seen below to the west of the road.

PARKING: At roadside

Plate 1. *River Aposelemis Pools, which vary from year to year, following the winter rains and water abstraction, attract a large variety of birds.*

Plate 2. *Moni Prevelli lies in an isolated position on the south coast and attracts migrant birds to the trees and scrub below the monastery.*

Plate 3. *View across to Akrotiri from Aptera with Souda Bay below. The area is a migration route as well as a fine viewpoint. Aptera was a city state commanding Souda Bay.*

Plate 4. *Agia Triada monastery drive on Akrotiri which can attract Scops Owl in the trees, and other migrants in the nearby fields and scrub. The monastery lies in a beautiful site planted with Olive trees, vineyards and Cypress trees.*

Plate 5. *Heraklion Power Station, showing the brackish spring pool, which provides water for the station.*

Plate 6. *Petres Gorge, illustrating why wet areas attract birds and other wildlife.*

Plate 7. *Elounda Old Salt Pans, a small area which attracts Little Egrets and other Herons in Spring and Autumn. Nearby was the Graeco-Roman town of Olous.*

Plate 8. *Seli Ambelou Pass, Lassithi, an excellent raptor watching spot especially for Lammergeier.*

Plate 9. *Georgioupolis Lake, showing the freshwater springs. Migrant birds feed at the lake in Spring and in Winter ducks, Coot and Moorhen feed here. Local resident birds feed and wash in the shallows where the springs emerge.*

TIME OF YEAR: Spring   Summer   Autumn   Winter
                    *   /   ?   ?

DESCRIPTION: The river has gone underground at the ford. Near to Perama there are a series of pools, sometimes polluted, which can be seen from the road above or reached by tracks from the ford, or from Perama.

BIRDS: Little Bittern, Little Egret, Purple Heron, Garganey, Little Ringed Plover, Little Stint, Common Sandpiper, Cuckoo, Hoopoe, Tree Pipit, Red-throated Pipit, Yellow Wagtail, White Wagtail, Thrush Nightingale, Orphean Warbler, Collared and Pied Flycatchers, Cetti's Warbler.

30 OMALOS PLATEAU AND SAMARIA GORGE.

LOCATION: The OMALOS PLATEAU lies 44 Km southwest of Chania.

PARKING: At road sides and at the car park at the mouth of the gorge.

TIME OF YEAR: Spring   Summer   Autumn   Winter
                    *   *   ?   /

DESCRIPTION: The road to the Plateau passes AGIA RESERVOIR, and climbs through orange groves, tree heather and pines and offers chances of many birds. The OMALOS PLATEAU is flat and is very good for flowers in Spring, with anemones, chinodoxa, tulips and peonies, as well as Woodlark, Tawny Pipit and Ortolan.

The SAMARIA GORGE is a National Park. There is now an entrance fee and the area is wardened to prevent entrance before the opening date of May 1st. The walk through the gorge is an 11 Km trek, which should only be undertaken by the well prepared through to Agia Roumeli. From here a regular boat service runs to Chora Sfakion. Accommodation

Map 30. OMALOS PLATEAU AND SAMARIA GORGE.

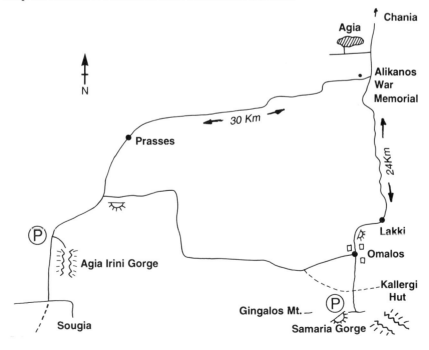

is also available at Agia Roumeli.

However, the area at the gorge top is a good viewpoint. Lammergeier can be seen from here if you are lucky. Mid to late morning is recommended. In the afternoon there have been regular reports from the area between Lakki and Omalos where the road is on top of the ridge check for Alpine Accentor around upper cafe wall.

The back route to OMALOS offers a chance to view raptors and to visit the AGIA IRINI GORGE. Turn off at the war memorial at Alikanos. After Prasses in 1.5.Km there is a junction on a ridge with views. Continue down hill for Ag. Irini. Turn east at the viewpoint for OMALOS. This road is rough in parts but also well surfaced nearer Omalos.

BIRDS: PLATEAU: Chukar, Woodlark, Black-eared Wheatear, Wheatear, Stonechat, Lammergeier, Raven, Buzzard, Bonelli's Eagle, Chough, Alpine Chough, Cirl Bunting.

GORGE: Short-toed Treecreeper, Rock Thrush, Golden Eagle, Lammergeier, Crag Martin, Dipper, Grey Wagtail, White Wagtail, Wren, Choughs.

31. PALEOCHORA.

LOCATION: On the south coast 77 km from Chania. There is a daily ferry service along the south coast to Sougia, Agia Roumeli and Chora Sfakion.

PARKING: On the roadsides and at the beach at Paleochora.

TIME OF YEAR: Spring   Summer   Autumn   Winter
                   *   ?   *   ?

DESCRIPTION: An area of scrub and small streams and a river mouth surrounding the small harbour town of PALEOCHORA. Paleochora is on a fortified promontory the river runs into the sea to the east, this coast is rocky. The fort area can be good for migrants. The beach to the west is sandy and small streams can pick up waders and migrants. The surrounding hillsides are also good for orchids and flowers.

BIRDS: Little Egret, Grey Heron, Little Bittern, Night Heron, Shag, Little Crake, Common Sandpiper, Wood and Green Sandpiper, Turnstone, Stonechat, Woodchat Shrike, Bee-eater, Golden Oriole, Kingfisher, Red-footed Falcon, Kestrel

Map 31. PALEOCHORA

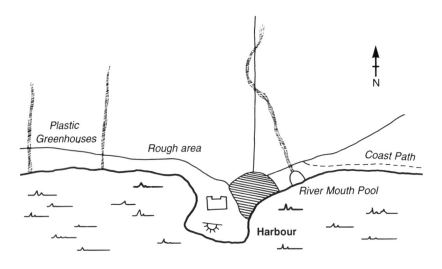

32. PETRES RIVER and GORGE.

LOCATION: On the main road 10 km west of Rethymnon between KM46 and KM47

PARKING: Going west on the seaward side after KM47.

TIME OF YEAR: Spring   Summer   Autumn   Winter
                       *   ?   *   ?

DESCRIPTION: A marshy area and pool on the landward side of the road which attracts a variety of herons, waders and migrants. A good watching point is the trig. point overlooking the pool on the east side of the river.

A chapel is under construction at the roadside entrance. The GORGE which is reached by a track on the eastern side of the river has breeding Griffon Vultures and possibly other birds of prey.

BIRDS: Little Egret, Grey Heron, Yellow Wagtail, Little Ringed Plover, Wood Sandpiper, Green Sandpiper, Tree Sparrow, White Wagtail, Chiff-chaff, Willow Warbler, Wood Warbler, Ruff, Griffon Vulture, Kestrel, Peregrine, Common Tern. Chukar, Woodlark, Wheatear, and Black-eared Wheatear, Lanner, Raven, Crag Martin.

Map 32. PETRES RIVER and GORGE.

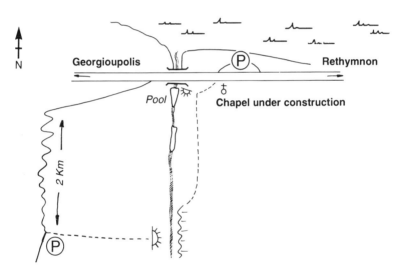

33. PHAESTOS, AGHIA TRIADA, and GEROPOTAMOS.

LOCATION: 62 km south from Heraklion, on the Plain of Messara.

PARKING: At the archaeological sites.

TIME OF YEAR: Spring   Summer   Autumn   Winter
                       *   ?   ?

DESCRIPTION: PHAESTOS carpark is a good viewpoint for raptors and the hillside below the archaeological site on the left has low scrub for warblers and pines for serins and finches. To the east is an area of open fields and damp pools. The hillside at PHAESTOS is good for orchids. Take the track to the right at the top of the car park in the direction of Aghia Triada. It is possible to follow red painted spots over the hillside to Aghia Triada. This is difficult to follow in parts, but it is an interesting walk. AGHIA TRIADA is 3 km further south. From the car park, the track, on either side of which many orchids grow, leads downhill towards orange groves and the river GEROPOTAMOS. At the ford follow the east bank towards the sea. The area then becomes a military zone.

BIRDS: Squacco Heron, Little Egret, Montagu's Harrier, Honey Buzzard, Buzzard, Golden Eagle, Griffon Vulture, Eleonora's Falcon, Greenshank, Black-eared Wheatear, Nightingale, Thrush Nightingale, Serin, Common Sandpiper, Wood Sandpiper, Marsh Sandpiper, Little Stint, Ruff, Great Snipe, Penduline Tit, Alpine Swift, Turtle Dove, Golden Oriole.

34. PLAKIAS and DAMNONI.

LOCATION: A small village resort in a large bay on the south coast, reached from Rethymnon through the KOURTALIOTIKO GORGE.

PARKING: Anywhere along the bay and at the eastern edge of the village.

TIME OF YEAR: Spring   Summer   Autumn   Winter
                   *   ?   ?   ?

DESCRIPTION: The village of Plakias stands in a large bay of the same name enclosed by a promentory. The promentory is good for Subalpine and Rüppells Warblers, Blue Rock Thrush and breeding Kestrels also endemic flowers. The bay attracts migrant flocks of Garganey and Herons. A small stream flows into the sea in the village. The stream area and the olive groves behind pick up migrants in Spring. A footpath starts at the stream and leads up to the KOTSIPHOS GORGE. This is a migration route through to the north and Golden Eagle, Griffon Vultures and Buzzard are also common. There are still rough fields and damp patches behind the bay to the east of the village but again development is threatened.

The Kakomouri headland is worth exploring. This lies to the east of the bay.

The nearby bay of DAMNONI to the east has been built on. There area still some areas of scrub but it is no longer productive. There are other bays further east which still have not suffered too much development, these can be reached on coastal footpaths and by road.

BIRDS: Griffon Vulture, Lammergeier, Montagu's Harrier, Hen Harrier, Pallid Harrier, Hobby, Glossy Ibis, Squacco Heron. Little Bittern, Wood Sandpiper, Common Sandpiper, Crane, Black-winged Stilt, Avocet, Garganey, Yellow Wagtail, Cuckoo, Woodcock, Scops Owl, Alpine Swift, Woodlark, Crested Lark, Woodchat & Masked Shrike, Great Reed Warbler, Subalpine Warbler, Rüppells Warbler, Blue Rock Thrush, Kestrel, Golden Eagle, Buzzard, Grey Heron, Night Heron, Fan-tailed Warbler, Nightingale, Hoopoe, Calandra Lark, Spanish Sparrow, Short-toed Lark.

35. PLATANES RIVER & GORGE.

LOCATION: Between Rethymnon on the old road from Rethymnon to Stavromenos. After the sign for Misiria is a white painted concrete bridge over the river on route to Platanes. The river mouth pool appears to be permanent.

PARKING: From Rethymnon on the old road, turn right before the bridge along road which runs under new road bridge. Also drive on to the cement works to view the river from the road. Park at the olive grove further on for the gorge.

River mouth POOL: On the Platanes side of the river follow signs to Snack Bar River.

TIME OF YEAR: Spring   Summer   Autumn   Winter
                   *   ?   *   ?

DESCRIPTION: A series of river pools from the cement works down to the beach. A walk up the road on west side of river leads to an interesting gorge with Lesser Kestrel, Hobby and Red-rumped Swallows.

Plate 10. Little Egret fishing from weed at 'River Center' near Heraklion Power Station. Other waders and Yellow Wagtails can be seen feeding here in spring.

Plate 11. Falasarna lies on the beautiful west coast. Blue Rock Thrush and Black-eared Wheatear breed here and migrants pass through in spring.

Plate 12. *Elounda, Saltpans and Spinalonga peninsula. Mediterranean Shearwaters can be seen in Mirabello Bay in windy weather. In the background is St. Johns Point an excellent viewpoint.*

Plate 13. *Turkish Bridge, over Megalopotamos, in the Moni Prevelli valley. Many migrants use the valley to feed in spring.*

Plate 14. *Petres River mouth pool has a good viewpoint looking down on the pool and south into the Petres Gorge.*

Plate 15. *Agia Reservoir near Chania is the best wetland area in the west attracting Duck, Herons, Terns and migrant passerines. Viewing is best from the pumping station in the morning and the dam in the afternoon.*

Plate 16. *Rethymnon beach and Fortezza, showing the areas which attract birds amongst the urban development.*

Plate 17. *Sitia harbour at the eastern end of Crete attracts Terns and Gulls and Mediterranean Shearwaters passing through travelling north in the spring.*

Above the cement works the river is clean but between the cement works and the concrete bridge the river is polluted. Below the bridge it is clear again with gravel banks and pools.

BIRDS: 3 species of Heron, Green and Wood Sandpiper, Little Ringed Plover, Little and Temminck's Stints, Greenshank, Redshank, Ruff, Common Snipe, Little Crake, Cetti's and Fan-tailed Warblers, Red-throated Pipit, Wheatear, Black-eared Wheatear, Golden Oriole, Scops Owl, Kestrel, Hobby, Red-rumped Swallow, Glossy Ibis, Collared Pratincole.

Map 35. PLATANES RIVER & GORGE

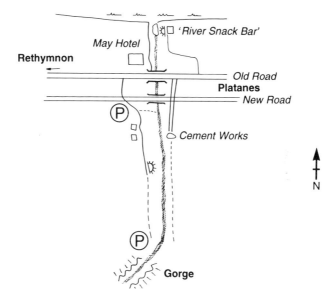

36. RETHYMNON OLD ROAD.

LOCATION: East of RETHYMNON on the old coast road.

PARKING: Hotel car parks, and roadsides.

TIME OF YEAR: Spring   Summe   Autumn   Winter
                   *   ?   *   ?

DESCRIPTION: Between the Adele Mare Hotel and the El Greco Hotel there are sandy beaches backed by sand dunes, and short grass and arable fields, alas there is continued encroaching development. Further along the road a pool is formed by a river at Stavromenos.

BIRDS: Glossy Ibis, Whinchat, Wheatear, Crested Lark, Short-toed Lark, Tawny, Tree and Red-throated Pipits, Woodchat Shrike, Fan-tailed Warbler, Yellow Wagtails, Black-tailed Godwit, Curlew, Little Ringed Plover, Booted Eagle, Marsh Harrier.

37. RETHYMNON PINES AND PROFITIS ELIAS CHAPEL.

LOCATION: Above RETHYMNON. Turn uphill signed to Ag.Irini.Continue steeply uphill passing under the bypass until an area of pines is reached on the left.

PARKING: On the left handside on a steep bend with steps up into the Pines, or up a steep concrete road, also on the left 100m further up the road. Parking on the narrow road is not recommended as service buses use this route.

TIME OF YEAR: Spring   Summer   Autumn   Winter
                         *   /   *   ?

DESCRIPTION: The Pines hold a variety of migrants and breeding birds, this is the only large area of pines on the north coast and it is a good magnet for migrants. The sides of the concrete track are good for orchids. The track across the road up to the chapel has resident warblers and birds use the rocky valley below as a migration route. There is a second section of Pines below the bypass. This area can be reached from the town. There are footpaths laid out through both areas of pines.

BIRDS: Migrants; Bee-eater, Roller, Warblers, Cuckoo, Firecrest, Pied Flycatcher, Collared Flycatcher, Redstart, Nightingale. Breeding; Chaffinch, Sardinian Warbler.

38. RETHYMNON BEACH & FORTEZZA.

LOCATION: In the centre of town. Follow signs to the beach or to the Fortezza.

PARKING: In Iroon Square or on the road behind the beach.

TIME OF YEAR: Spring   Summer   Autumn   Winter
                         *   /   *   ?

DESCRIPTION: Rethymnon Beach is backed by rough grass and sand which can hold migrant waders early in the season or in bad weather. Past the harbour under the Fort is an area of rocks where Little Egrets and gulls roost. To the east of the beach, at a long concrete promentory is an outfall which can attract Mediterranean gulls and Sandwich Terns in Spring.
The Fortezza (Entrance fee) area has pines and scrub and can be good for migrants.

BIRDS: Little Stint, Curlew Sandpiper, Ruff, Wood Sandpiper, Common Sandpiper, Common Tern, Little Tern, Gull-billed Tern, Mediterranean Gull, Little Egret, Herring Gull, Red-throated Pipit, Serin, Black-eared Wheatear.

39. SELINARI GORGE and OLD ROAD TO AGIOS NIKOLAOS.

LOCATION: Just east of Malia both old and new roads pass through SELINARI GORGE to Agios Nikolaos.
For OLD ROAD turn off the new main road travelling east at KM177 at the beginning of the gorge.

PARKING: In lay-bys.

TIME OF YEAR: Spring   Summer   Autumn   Winter
                         *   /   *   ?

DESCRIPTION: Interesting road with suitable stopping places, to see birds of prey over Selinari Gorge. There are rubbish dumps at several points and despite dumping at the pool at Limnes it can have migrant waders and terns on passage.

BIRDS: Griffon Vulture, Golden Eagle, Kestrel, Buzzard, Cuckoo, Black Tern, Green Sandpiper, Herring Gull, Woodchat Shrike, Red-backed Shrike.

40. SKOUTELONAS RIVER. (River Spiliakos).

LOCATION: On main road between Chania and Kastelli Kassimou. East of Kolimbari between KM22 and KM23. The west bank of the river is Kolimbari and the east bank is Rapaniana.

PARKING: At bridge on the north side of the road, or drive down to the mouth of the river on the west side signposted to Irini Beach Apartments

TIME OF YEAR: Spring   Summer   Autumn   Winter
                        *   /   *   ?

DESCRIPTION: There are usually reeds (sometimes cut) below the bridge. Further towards the sea the river opens to a pool and lagoon. The road west of the river, gives good views and it is possible to drive down and use the car as a hide. There are tracks to the west and east of the river, past the apartments, which lead into interesting shore fields. Unfortunately building developments are taking place along this part of the coast.

BIRDS: Hirundines, Herons, Marsh Harrier, Fan-tailed Warbler, Yellow Wagtails, Spanish Sparrow, Common Sandpiper, Snipe, Curlew Sandpiper, Wood Sandpiper, Stonechat, Northern Wheatear, Red-throated Pipit, Short-toed Lark.

Map 40. SKOUTELONAS RIVER.(River Spiliakos)

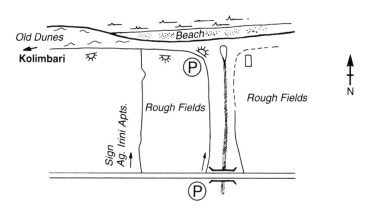

41. SOUDA BAY CEMETERY.

LOCATION: The British War Cemetery situated at the head of Souda Bay nine km east of CHANIA. Turn off at KM9 from the main road. Or follow signs to Souda from Chania town centre. In Souda follow signs to British Cemetery.

PARKING: At olive trees at the entrance to the cemetery.

TIME OF YEAR: Spring   Summer   Autumn   Winter
                         *   ?   *   ?

DESCRIPTION: The cemetery is a well kept garden surrounded by trees. The olive grove at the carpark and the eucalyptus trees can be busy with feeding migrants in Spring. The bay and shore can also be interesting. View from the eastern end of the wall.

BIRDS: Little Egret, Grey Heron, Osprey, Sandwich Tern, Redstart, Wryneck, Bonelli's Warbler, Black-eared Wheatear, Swift, Alpine Swift, Cuckoo, Tree Pipit, Woodchat and Red-backed Shrikes, Wood Warbler, Chaffinch, Sardinian Warbler, Tree Sparrow.

42. TAVRONITIS RIVER.

LOCATION: 20 km west of Chania. After passing the barracks on the left, there is a sharp bend and then the road crosses the river.

PARKING: For Upstream. After the bridge travelling west or on the east side of the river off the rough track.

For Downstream at Charidimos Apts.

TIME OF YEAR: Spring   Summer   Autumn   Winter
                   *   ?   *   ?

DESCRIPTION: The river is very good for migrants. Upstream: Cross over the bridge to the eastside and follow the track northwards to find pools and sandbanks where migrants rest.

Downstream: Drive down past the works and follow the dirt road towards the sea. P at Charidimos Apts. Check the farm fields and the small wood to the west. Walk east at the stony beach towards the river mouth. In amongst Giant Reed is a rivermouth pool.

The reeds and military area to the east of the river towards Maleme attract Marsh Harriers and Black Kite. Do not attempt to enter this area.

BIRDS: Garganey, Ferruginous Duck, Snipe, Red-rumped Swallow, Swift, Wood, Common and Green Sandpipers, Black Kite, Marsh Harrier, Little Ringed Plover, Ringed Plover, Osprey. Cetti's Warbler, Great Reed Warbler, Fan-tailed Warbler, White Wagtail, Crested Lark.

Map 42. TAVRONITIS RIVER

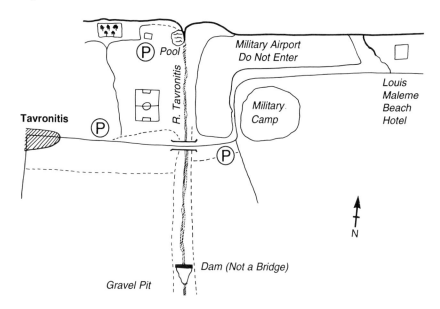

43. THRAPSANO POOL.

LOCATION: On the east side of THRAPSANO near KASTELLI.

PARKING: At the Pool. Turn off by a new church on the east edge of Thrapsano. Follow the dirt track for 1Km to the pool.

TIME OF YEAR: Spring   Summer   Autumn   Winter
                   *   /   ?   *

DESCRIPTION: A concrete dammed irrigation pool which is filled by winter rains. Water levels may vary. It currently have some surrounding scrub on the south side.The pool has been enlarged in Autumn 1995.

BIRDS: Little Egret, Little Bittern, Night Heron, Snipe, Wood Sandpiper, Moorhen,

Black-winged Stilt, Little Stint, Common Sandpiper, Scops Owl, Red-rumped Swallow, Sedge Warbler, Great Reed Warbler.

Map 43. THRAPSANO POOL

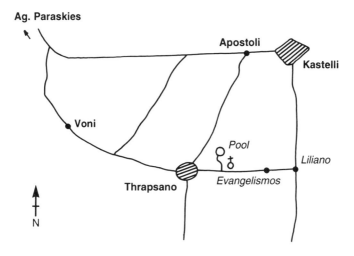

SURVEY OF CRETE RECORDS 1986-1995

Numbers denote total numbers of birds seen over the years 1986 to 1992
*Some records for 1984, 1985 and 1993 and 1994 are also included if they indicate additional species.
* Recorded as present per (C&JH) from November 1990-March 1995.
◆Records without totals.

Little Grebe *Tachybaptus ruficollis*
Resident in small numbers, young recorded in 1994. Frequent passage migrant.

J	F	M	A	M	J	J	A	S	O	N	D
14	1	58	150	43	3	7	6	3	54	5	22

Great Crested Grebe *Podiceps cristatus*
Rare winter visitor

J	F	M	A	M	J	J	A	S	O	N	D
*	*	2	2								

1987 1 on Souda Bay 28.3.1987 (J.Osborne, SC et al.)
1990 1 in winter plumage Lake Kournas 7.4.1990 (J Nadin).
1992 2 in Ierapetra harbour on 20.3.1992 (C&JH).
1993 1 Elounda 27.1.93. (C&JH).

Black-necked Grebe *Podiceps nigricollis*
Frequent passage migrant and winter visitor.

J	F	M	A	M	J	J	A	S	O	N	D
16	213	124	161	5				14	30	15	155

Cory's Shearwater *Calonectris diomedea*
Passage Migrant. Breeding on offshore islands.
Common summer visitor March-October.

J	F	M	A	M	J	J	A	S	O	N	D
		30	1000	122	40		2000	62	2000		

Mediterranean Shearwater *Puffinus yelkouan*
Passage migrant. Summer visitor.

J	F	M	A	M	J	J	A	S	O	N	D
	1500	2280	13	43			6	4	16	5	

Storm Petrel *Hydrobates pelagicus*
Vagrant. Only 4 records. No records since 1975.

Cormorant *Phalacrocorax carbo*
Rare passage migrant. Winter visitor.

J	F	M	A	M	J	J	A	S	O	N	D
27	16	6	34	16			1	53	15	1	18

Shag *Phalacrocorax aristotelis*
Rare Resident

J	F	M	A	M	J	J	A	S	O	N	D
	5	5	26	10			12	3			*

Pygmy Cormorant *Phalacrocorax pygmeus*
Vagrant. Only 2 records (4 birds) since 1986.

J	F	M	A	M	J	J	A	S	O	N	D
		3							1		

1988 1 at Almyros 16.10. 1988. (Ivan Nethercoat)
1989 3 Almyros including 1 in breeding plumage feeding at river mouth 22.3.1989. (Graham Clark)

White Pelican *Pelecanus onocrotalus*
Resident up to 5 tame birds since 1989 at Ag. Nikolaos, Sitia, Sougia and possibly Ierapetra? The origin of these birds is obscure.

Bittern *Botaurus stellaris*
Rare passage migrant.

J	F	M	A	M	J	J	A	S	O	N	D
4	1		11	15						1	1

Little Bittern *Ixobrychus minutus*
Regular passage migrant in small numbers.

J	F	M	A	M	J	J	A	S	O	N	D
		2	38	48			1	5	6		

Night Heron *Nycticorax nycticorax*
Frequent Passage Migrant

J	F	M	A	M	J	J	A	S	O	N	D
			393	83	1		22	103	21		

Squacco Heron *Ardeola ralliodes*
Frequent passage migrant, a few birds summer.

J	F	M	A	M	J	J	A	S	O	N	D
		2	560	214	13	5	80	68	4		

Cattle Egret *Bubulcus ibis*
Vagrant 2 records.
1986 1 on river Geros 28th April 1986.(P.K. & B.A. Dedicoat)
1987 The long dead remains of 1 Gouves lagoon 16th October 1987.(D. Ireland)

Little Egret *Egretta garzetta*
Common passage migrant Mid March -early May, Mid August-early October.
A few birds winter and summer.

J	F	M	A	M	J	J	A	S	O	N	D
*	*	◆	◆	◆	6	◆	◆	◆	◆	1	◆

Great White Egret *Egretta alba*
Rare passage migrant. Recorded April-May and August-September, and rarely March & October.

Grey Heron *Ardea cinerea*
Common passage migrant Spring peak-April, a few birds may Summer.
Autumn peak-September, October.

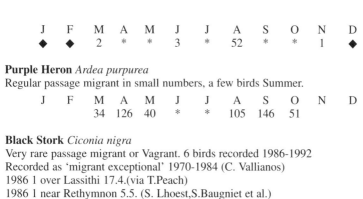

J	F	M	A	M	J	J	A	S	O	N	D
◆	◆	2	*	*	3	*	52	*	*	1	◆

Purple Heron *Ardea purpurea*
Regular passage migrant in small numbers, a few birds Summer.

J	F	M	A	M	J	J	A	S	O	N	D
		34	126	40	*	*	105	146	51		

Black Stork *Ciconia nigra*
Very rare passage migrant or Vagrant. 6 birds recorded 1986-1992
Recorded as 'migrant exceptional' 1970-1984 (C. Vallianos)
1986 1 over Lassithi 17.4.(via T.Peach)
1986 1 near Rethymnon 5.5. (S. Lhoest,S.Baugniet et al.)
1986 1 soaring over Hamezi west of Sitia 6.5. (S. Edwards)
1986 1 Spili beginning of May (SJ Denny)
1986 1 near Roumeli end of May. (J. Wakenshaw)
1991 1 at Mylo river mid morning 18.4.(SC et al.)

White Stork *Ciconia ciconia*
Rare passage migrant recorded April, May, August and October.

Glossy Ibis *Plegadis falcinellus*
Regular passage migrant.

J	F	M	A	M	J	J	A	S	O	N	D
		79	1120	7			575	84	39		

Spoonbill *Platalea leucorodia*
Rare passage migrant, a total of 9 birds since 1986, all April.

Greater Flamingo *Phoenicopterus ruber*
Rare passage migrant

J	F	M	A	M	J	J	A	S	O	N	D
		1	5	18							

Mute Swan *Cygnus olor*
Vagrant
*1993 1 at Elounda Saltpans 27.1. (C&J Henshall)
*1994 Influx up to 15 during January remaining into spring, April. (CJH, SC et al, D.Ireland et al. featured on Kriti TV)
2 Rethymnon Harbour 8.10. & 1 there 15.10.(PM)
*1995 2 April & May Agia reservoir.

White-fronted Goose *Anser albifrons*
1992 1 at Ierapetra reservoir April.(J, Steele)
1993 1 at Ierapetra reservoir 1.4. (C& JH)

Greylag Goose *Anser anser*
1992 & 1993 as above paired with *Anser albifrons*.

Shelduck *Tadorna tadorna*
Vagrant? Only 1 record
1992 1 at Ierapetra reservoir 21st January 1992. (C&J Henshall).

Wigeon *Anas penelope*
Frequent winter visitor

J	F	M	A	M	J	J	A	S	O	N	D
101	24	11	8	1				1	12	18	

Gadwall *Anas strepera*
Rare/Frequent winter visitor.

J	F	M	A	M	J	J	A	S	O	N	D
*	*	*						2	2	13	*

Teal *Anas crecca*
No recent records since 1976. Then 3 records of 10 in 1993. Now recorded as common winter visitor.

J	F	M	A	M	J	J	A	S	O	N	D
*	*	*	2					32	61		

Mallard *Anas platyrhynchos*
Small numbers winter, evidence of Autumn passage August and October.

J	F	M	A	M	J	J	A	S	O	N	D
41	21	31	17				200		238	108	

Pintail *Anas acuta*
Frequent winter (peak January) and Autumn passage. Migrant during October.

J	F	M	A	M	J	J	A	S	O	N	D
142	69	21	75	10				7	895	15	4

Garganey *Anas querquedula*
Regular passage migrant. Spring and Autumn.

J	F	M	A	M	J	J	A	S	O	N	D
		26	1140	32				39	44	138	

Shoveler *Anas clypeata*
Rare winter visitor. Scarce on Spring passage.

J	F	M	A	M	J	J	A	S	O	N	D
11		8	12	2						2	

Marbled Duck *Marmaronetta angustirostris*
Vagrant. Total of 24 birds all during April.
1984 20+ flew into Plaka Bay 11.4.1984.(I.Monro & Monro).
1988 Georgioupolis Lake 2 for several days up to 18.4.1988.(J. Steele)
1991 2 Georgioupolis Lake 7.4.1991. (D.Townsend)

Red-crested Pochard *Netta rufina*
No records between 1977 and 1992.
1993 3 at Ierapetra reservoir 27.1.1993(C&J Henshall)

Common Pochard *Aythya ferina*
Winter visitor in small numbers

J	F	M	A	M	J	J	A	S	O	N	D
244	90	31	4				9			254	18

Ferruginous Duck *Aythya nyroca*
Rare winter visitor and Spring migrant

J	F	M	A	M	J	J	A	S	O	N	D
1	2	4	15	6	1				◆	23	

Tufted Duck *Aythya fuligula*
Scarce /Rare winter visitor

J	F	M	A	M	J	J	A	S	O	N	D
16	14		6	2							5

Red-breasted Merganser *Mergus serrator*
Vagrant 1 record. 3rd record for Crete.
*1994 1 female on the sea off Analypsis, Hersonissos 26.1.1994 (C&JH)

Honey Buzzard *Pernis apivorus*
Scarce passage migrant April and May, Rare in autumn.

J	F	M	A	M	J	J	A	S	O	N	D
			32	35			2	2	3	1	

Black Kite *Milvus migrans*
Scarce passage migrant mainly April. Rare in autumn.

J	F	M	A	M	J	J	A	S	O	N	D
			41	11			2	2	4		

Red Kite *Milvus milvus*
Vagrant only 4 records(6 birds)1986-92
*1984 1 behind Kotsiphos Gorge April 1984 (L. Chilton et al).
1988 2 behind Kotsiphos 12.4.88.(SC&JJC et al)
1988 2 on route to Falasarna 16.4.88 (B. Illingworth et al.)
1989 1 near Milatos 14.4.1989.(W. Mann)
1989 1 Falasarna in first half of October 1989.(D. M. Morisson)

Lammergeier *Gypaetus barbatus*
Resident, possibly 6-10 pairs? Most records Dikti & Lefka Ori mountain ranges.

Egyptian Vulture *Neophron percnopterus*
Very rare passage migrant. Records mainly from Kritsa to Sitia Mountains.
1970-1984 C.Vallianos no details on dates (Vallianos 1984)
1980 2 between Agia Roumeli and Chora Sfakion 3 10.1980 (W.Thiede).
1986 April/early May 1 seen between Gournia and Sitia (J. Barker)
1986 1 juvenile seen Kato Zakro Gorge 22.4.1986.(S.Lhoest, S.Baugniet)
1994 1 Kallergi Refuge 3.4.1994.(RDWilson).

Griffon Vulture *Gyps fulvus*
Common resident in gorges, throughout all but the eastern end of the island. Flock sizes from 3-35.

Black Vulture *Aegypius monachus*
No recent records since 1976.

Short-toed Eagle *Circaetus gallicus*
Scarce passage migrant only 16+ records 1986-94

Marsh Harrier *Circus aeruginosus*
Frequent Spring passage migrant April to early May. A few do winter.

J	F	M	A	M	J	J	A	S	O	N	D
3	2	7	96	27		1	2	6	5	1	

Hen Harrier *Circus cyaneus*
Very rare passage migrant during April & May, and a few do winter.

J	F	M	A	M	J	J	A	S	O	N	D
1	1		4	*					1		*

Pallid Harrier *Circus macrourus*
Very rare passage migrant during April.

Montagu's Harrier *Circus pygargus*
Scarce passage migrant mainly April.

J	F	M	A	M	J	J	A	S	O	N	D
			35	7							

Goshawk *Accipiter gentilis*
Very rare passage migrant April, May & October.

Sparrowhawk *Accipiter nisus*
Frequent resident and scarce passage migrant during April,

J	F	M	A	M	J	J	A	S	O	N	D
1	*		31	2	*	2	1	1	5	3	1

Levant Sparrowhawk *Accipiter brevipes*
Vagrant not recorded before 1989. 4 records (5 birds).

1989 1 male and 1 female near Anatoli 23.3.89.(G.Clark).
1990 1 Phaestos 24.8.90 (AJ Richards)
1991 1 Gortys 6.4.1991 (D.Townsend).
1992 1 Malia 8.4.1992 (SC et al).

Buzzard *Buteo buteo*
Resident and common but thinly distributed.

Long-legged Buzzard *Buteo rufinus*
Rare passage migrant mainly April and May.

J	F	M	A	M	J	J	A	S	O	N	D
		1	15	8	1			2	3		

Golden Eagle *Aquila chrysaetos*
Resident. Widely distributed, increasing? 12-14 sites in 1993/1994.

Booted Eagle *Hieraaetus pennatus*
Scarce passage migrant. A few birds winter. Resident.

J	F	M	A	M	J	J	A	S	O	N	D
		1	42	12	1			3	2	7	2	1

Bonelli's Eagle *Hieraaetus fasciatus*
Resident, rare and thinly distributed over the island.

J	F	M	A	M	J	J	A	S	O	N	D
	*		2	10	1	2		4	1		

Osprey *Pandion haliaetus*
Rare passage migrant mainly April-early May.

J	F	M	A	M	J	J	A	S	O	N	D
		1	15	5		1		1	1		

Lesser Kestrel *Falco naumanni*
Rare passage migrant. Summer Visitor. Most records from Rethymnon-Plakias eastwards.

J	F	M	A	M	J	J	A	S	O	N	D
			6	5				14			

Kestrel *Falco tinnunculus*
Common resident. Passage migrant.

Red-footed Falcon *Falco vespertinus*
Regular passage migrant. Late April-May. Very few Autumn records - August.

Merlin *Falco columbarius*
Very rare passage migrant April - May and possibly October.

Hobby *Falco subbuteo*
Scarce passage migrant April-May. Few Autumn records.

J	F	M	A	M	J	J	A	S	O	N	D
*		1	27	18	4		2	3	3		

Eleanora's Falcon *Falco eleanorae*
Common Summer visitor. Some birds possibly passage migrants. Arrives early April and widespread May - October. Singles until early November.

Lanner *Falco biarmicus*
Scarce resident?

J	F	M	A	M	J	J	A	S	O	N	D
			1	3					1		

Saker *Falco cherrug*
1981 1 record near Katheron plateau (EDH Johnson)

Peregrine *Falco peregrinus*
Resident, also passage migrant. April-early May.

J	F	M	A	M	J	J	A	S	O	N	D
4	1	2	62	30	4		6	4	14	3	*

Chukar *Alectoris chukar*
Resident and frequent.

Quail *Coturnix coturnix*
Passage migrant. A few summer visitors.

J	F	M	A	M	J	J	A	S	O	N	D
		1	20	12	2		1				

Water Rail Rallus *aquaticus*
Resident in small numbers and partial migrant.

J	F	M	A	M	J	J	A	S	O	N	D
3	1	2	1					*		2	6

Spotted Crake *Porzana porzana*
Scarce passage migrant during April, May & October.

Little Crake *Porzana parva*
Frequent passage migrant in small numbers April - May.

J	F	M	A	M	J	J	A	S	O	N	D
		6	70	48						1	

Baillon's Crake *Porzana pusilla*
Very rare passage migrant, April. 9 records 1986-92.

Corncrake *Crex crex*
Vagrant. Only 1 record 1986-1992.
1986 1 Malia early April 1986 (P. Raynor & Raynor)

Moorhen *Gallinula chloropus*
Resident. Common passage migrant with a peak in late March/April. A few pairs breed, small numbers winter.

Coot *Fulica atra*
Resident and Common Winter Visitor. September - March.

Common Crane *Grus grus*
Rare Spring Passage Migrant in April.

Oystercatcher *Haematopus ostralegus*
Vagrant. 1 record (5 birds)
1992 5 Georgioupolis Lake 6.10.1992.(C&J Henshall).

Black-winged Stilt *Himantopus himantopus*
Frequent passage migrant April-early May. Small numbers August.

J	F	M	A	M	J	J	A	S	O	N	D
		3	202	36	1		63				?

Avocet *Recurvirostra avosetta*
Very rare passage migrant March - May.
*1976 21 flying offshore Almyros 23.8.1976. (CRG)
*1977 1 River Platis, Ag. Galini 1st May 1977 (C.Davies)
1987 1 at Gouves lagoon 25.3. 31.3. and 2.4. (NNT tour, I. Loades, SCet al)
1988 6 Plakias beach 12.4.1988. Later the same day 3 there.(SC et al)
1991 1 Ierapetra reservoir 1.5.1991.(M.Coath)

Stone Curlew *Burhinus oedicnemus*
Passage migrant in small numbers during April.
Vagrant winter, 1 record December.

Cream-coloured Coursor *Cursorius curser*
Very rare vagrant. First record for Crete and 4th for Greece.
1993 From 31.3. to 4.4.1993. Gouves lagoon, beach by river Aposelemis mouth.(John Metcalf) (C&JHenshall).

Collared Pratincole *Glareola pratincola*
Scarce but regular Spring passage migrant.

J	F	M	A	M	J	J	A	S	O	N	D
			121	5							

Little Ringed Plover *Charadrius dubius*
Regular passage migrant. Late March with peak in April. Evidence of return passage August. Breeding recorded at several sites along the north coast.
Last records 28.9.1994, 26.10.1993. Nov.(C&JH) Recorded March-Nov.

Ringed Plover *Charadrius hiaticula*
Scarce passage migrant mainly April.

J	F	M	A	M	J	J	A	S	O	N	D
		2	35	12			2		4		

Kentish Plover *Charadrius alexandrinus*
Rare passage migrant. April and May. 1 record February 1995 (SC).

Greater Sand Plover *Charadrius leschenaultii*
Vagrant, 1989, 3 and once 4 at Hotel Stella village, Analypsis from 29.7. to 18.8.1989
(L.Rudy & Rudy)

Caspian Plover *Charadrius asiaticus*
Vagrant, 1 record April 1990.
1990 1 Malia 23-24. 4.1990. (Granville Potter, Robert Oades)

Dotterel *Charadrius morinellus*
Vagrant, 1 record April 1986.
1986 1 walking along main beach road between Rethymnon and Perivolia very early in the
morning 20.4.1986.(T.Dougall)

Pacific Golden Plover *Pluvialis fulva*
Vagrant.
*1985 1 on rocks of El Greco Hotel, Rethymnon 12.4.1985. (J.Ogle)
1989 a single bird in winter plumage at Damnoni beach 15.4.1989. (D.Ireland, J. Osborne
et al)

Golden Plover *Pluvialis apricaria*
Very rare, winter and April and May.
*1981 1 Gouves lagoon and Aposelemis river mouth 15.4.1981 Southern race.(SC & JJC)
*1985 1 on 15th & 17th in winter plumage on 'plover rocks' on coast near El.Greco,
Rethymnon. (J. Barker).
1988 1 in winter plumage Gouves lagoon 7.5.1988 (J.Barker)
1993 1 Malia 22.11.1993 (C&J Henshall).
1994 1 Koutsounari 9.11.1994. (C&J Henshall).

Grey Plover *Pluvialis squatarola*
Rare only 6 records 1986-1992
*1985 off El Greco Hotel, Rethymnon 17.4.1985(J.Barker)
1986 1 river Aposelemis 8.5.1986. (PK Dedicoat)
1987 1 in summer plumage Elounda 19.5.1987 (Keith Bannister)
1988 1 in summer plumage Gouves lagoon 7.5.1988 (J.Barker)
1988 1 Elounda 19.10.1988 (Ivan Nethercoat)
1994 2 Souda Bay, 11.4.-17.4.1994.(S.Foster. et al).

Spur-winged Plover. *Hoplopterus spinosus*
Vagrant. Only 1 record April 1992.
1992 1 at Sitia river for several hours during the morning of 13.4.1992. (J. Scivyer, SC et
al.)

Sociable Plover *Chettusia gregaria*
Vagrant. Only 1 record April 1986.

1986 1 at Gouves lagoon 29.4.1986. Photographed by Ray Smith. (R.Smith, SC, University of Kent tour et al)

White-tailed Plover *Chettusia leucura*
Vagrant. only 2-3 records 1986-1994.
1986 1 on muddy track at Malia 25.4.1986. (M I Macdonald)
1986 1 Creta Sun hotel log April 1986. (no details) (Same bird?)
*1994 1 all day at Elounda saltpans 6.4.1994. Photographed and description submitted to recorder for Greece. (P.Mackinder, S.Feeney, SC.) [M.Richardson & M.Langridge Photographs.]

Lapwing *Vanellus vanellus*
Rare winter visitor.

J	F	M	A	M	J	J	A	S	O	N	D
*	12	2	2							7	

Knot *Calidris canutus*
No recent records. 2 records 1974 and 1979.

Sanderling *Calidris alba*
Scarce passage migrant.

J	F	M	A	M	J	J	A	S	O	N	D
			22	16							

Little Stint *Calidris minuta*
Common passage migrant late March-May. Peak in April, small numbers Summer, Autumn passage, August-Sept.Winter records of singles January and December.

Temminck's Stint *Calidris temminckii*
Scarce passage migrant.

J	F	M	A	M	J	J	A	S	O	N	D
			22	27			1				

Curlew Sandpiper *Calidris ferruginea*
Frequent passage migrant April-May.(peak May).

J	F	M	A	M	J	J	A	S	O	N	D
		1	45	102			*	2	5	1	

Dunlin *Calidris alpina*
Scarce passage migrant April. Winter visitor

J	F	M	A	M	J	J	A	S	O	N	D
*	6	2	26	5		1	5	4	4	4	51

Broad-billed Sandpiper *Limicola falcinellus*
Vagrant, one record August.(Record pending)
1990 1 Damnoni beach 18.8.1990 (AJ Richards)

Ruff *Philomachus pugnax*
Regular passage migrant March-May (peak April).

J	F	M	A	M	J	J	A	S	O	N	D
	4	49	245	134	2			*	1		

Jack Snipe *Lymnocryptes minimus*
Vagrant only 1 record.
1988 1 freshly dead Plakias beach 16th April 1988 (D. Ireland et al).

Common Snipe *Gallinago gallinago*
Regular passage migrant in small numbers, April.
Scarce winter visitor October-March.

J	F	M	A	M	J	J	A	S	O	N	D
1	2	15	24	8			2	1	60	6	3

Great Snipe *Gallinago media*
Rare passage migrant April-May. 2 records pre 1986 in autumn(CRG) & (JRP)

Woodcock *Scolopax rusticola*
Vagrant, only 2 records.
1985 1 Malia 21.4.1985. (David Boertmann)
1987 1 Plakias April/May 1987 (via Lance Chilton)

Black-tailed Godwit *Limosa limosa*
Rare/uncommon/passage migrant March-April.

J	F	M	A	M	J	J	A	S	O	N	D
		*	*	1	1						

Whimbrel *Numenius phaeopus*
Rare passage migrant April-May.
1994 1 Tersonas pond 31.3. 1994.(RD Wilson).

Curlew *Numenius arquata*
Rare passage migrant April. 3-5 Autumn records.

Spotted Redshank *Tringa erythropus*
Very rare passage migrant March, April-May.

J	F	M	A	M	J	J	A	S	O	N	D
		14	*	*			*	1	4		

Common Redshank *Tringa totanus*
Scarce/frequent passage migrant March-May.
Winter visitor in small numbers October-January.

J	F	M	A	M	J	J	A	S	O	N	D
3		14	41	11			7	1	19	11	

Marsh Sandpiper *Tringa stagnatilis*
Uncommon/Scarce passage migrant, mainly April.

J	F	M	A	M	J	J	A	S	O	N	D
			5	29			1				

Greenshank *Tringa nebularia*
Regular passage migrant, small numbers late March-May.

J	F	M	A	M	J	J	A	S	O	N	D
		5	110	28			1			1	

Green Sandpiper *Tringa ochropus*
Regular passage migrant March-early May and late July to early September.
A few birds winter.

J	F	M	A	M	J	J	A	S	O	N	D
3	2	35	84	11		2	73	66			1

Wood Sandpiper *Tringa glareola*
Common passage migrant April-May (peak April). Evidence of return passage August.

J	F	M	A	M	J	J	A	S	O	N	D
		8	365+	198	*		43	76	1	1	

Common Sandpiper *Actitis hypoleucos*
Common passage migrant peak April. Return passage small numbers August-September.
A few birds winter.

J	F	M	A	M	J	J	A	S	O	N	D
4	5	5	150+	15	*	2	56	34	4	2	2

Turnstone *Arenaria interpres*
Rare. Only 18 birds since 1986. All during May. Then 2 in April in 1993 & 1994.
Aug/Sept (C&JH).

Red-necked Phalarope *Phalaropus lobatus*
Vagrant. 1 record 1979. No recent records.

Arctic Skua *Stercorarius parasiticus*
Vagrant. 1 record 1928. No recent records.

Great Black-headed Gull *Larus ichthyaetus*
Vagrant 6 records. 4 recent records.
* 1981 1 Heraklion harbour 13.4.1981 Adult winter (SC & JJC)
1986 1 Heraklion power station roost 1st winter one date between 16th-30th May 1986 (J. Wakenshaw)
1987 1 immature flew along beach just west of Petres Gorge 18.4.1987 (D.Townsend).
1988 A second year Gouves 13.4.1988 (D.T.Ireland).

Mediterranean Gull *Larus melanocephalus*
Rare winter and Spring visitor. All non-breeding birds.

J	F	M	A	M	J	J	A	S	O	N	D
1	20	82	6						4		*

Little Gull *Larus minutus*
Rare passage migrant mainly immatures March-early May.

J	F	M	A	M	J	J	A	S	O	N	D
		5	19	4					1		

Black-headed Gull *Larus ridibundus*
Regular winter visitor Sept/October-April.

Slender-billed Gull *Larus genei*
Vagrant, Total of 7 records. 2 recent records.
1987 1 Sitia Harbour no specific date between 23.3.-6.4.1987 (W T Appleyard)

1989 A party of 11, 7th May 1989 Plakias Bay (E Barnes)

Audouin's Gull *Larus audouinii*
Locally common in Winter. Passage Migrant. Resident in small numbers on islands?

Common Gull *Larus canus*
Vagrant. 2 records.
1983 2nd record (P Weesie via Vallianos 1984)
1986 1 Vai, Toplou 22.4.1986 (SL. Ja VE via Bruxelles Aves Tour)

Lesser Black-backed Gull *Larus fuscus*
Passage migrant in small numbers mainly April, a few may Winter.

Yellow-legged Herring Gull *Larus cachinnans michahellis*
Widespread. No large roosts.

Kittiwake *Rissa tridactyla*
Vagrant, 2 recent records.
1989. 1 first winter bird during southerly gale 6.4.1989 (T. Dougall & G. Arbuthnot)
*1994 1 at Aposelemis river 2. & 4.3.1994 (C&J Henshall).

Gull-billed Tern *Gelochelidon nilotica*
Scarce passage migrant, mainly April. (1 party of 16)

J	F	M	A	M	J	J	A	S	O	N	D
		27	4	1					2		

Caspian Tern *Sterna caspia*
Rare passage migrant. Winter visitor.

J	F	M	A	M	J	J	A	S	O	N	D
		4	4					4	3		2

Sandwich Tern *Sterna sandvicensis*
Frequent passage migrant late March-April, few Aug.-Oct. Wintering?

J	F	M	A	M	J	J	A	S	O	N	D
3	13	109	1				1	11	6		

Common Tern *Sterna hirundo*
Scarce Spring passage migrant.

J	F	M	A	M	J	J	A	S	O	N	D
			17	1							

Little Tern *Sterna albifrons*
Rare Spring passage migrant.

J	F	M	A	M	J	J	A	S	O	N	D
			6	1							

Whiskered Tern *Chlidonias hybridus*
Scarce passage migrant April-early June.

J	F	M	A	M	J	J	A	S	O	N	D
		15	18	7	3						

Black Tern *Chlidonias niger*
Rare Spring passage migrant.

J	F	M	A	M	J	J	A	S	O	N	D
			4	3		1					

White-winged Black Tern *Chlidonias leucopterus*
Scarce passage migrant April-early May.
1990 c.60 recorded.

J	F	M	A	M	J	J	A	S	O	N	D
			c.72	39					1		

Rock Dove *Columba livia*
Resident in small numbers in the larger gorges.
1992 Party of 100 recorded January 1992.

Stock Dove *Columba oenas*
Rare passage migrant, only 9 records 1986-94.

Wood Pigeon *Columba palumbus*
Resident frequent but recorded as common some years, April and May.

Collared Dove *Streptopelia decaocto*
Rare resident restricted to Rethymnon until 1989. Evidence of a spread in 1990 mainly along north coast but first record in the south at Frangocastello. Continues to spread.

Turtle Dove *Streptopelia turtur*
Regular passage migrant scarce summer visitor. Spring passage April-May; Occasional June records. Few Autumn records Aug/Sept.

Great Spotted Cuckoo *Clamator glandarius*
Vagrant, 2 records.
1987 1 in late April flying over the reeds at Almyros. (T. Peach & Peach)
*1994. 1 in Sitia 8.9.1994. (C&JH)

Cuckoo *Cuculus canorus*
Regular passage migrant. April-early May.

J	F	M	A	M	J	J	A	S	O	N	D
			107	17							

Barn Owl *Tyto alba*
Rare resident, recorded most years, and in most months.

Scops Owl *Otus scops*
Fairly common summer visitor and rare resident.
Winter: 2 Argyroupolis 30.11. and 3 there 11.12.

Little Owl *Athene noctua*
Vagrant or very rare resident, only 1, record April 1989.

Long-eared Owl *Asio otus*
Vagrant, but there were 3 in a taxidermist's in Chania in October 1995. 7 records. Most recent 1981.

Nightjar *Caprimulgus europaeus*
Very Rare passage migrant mainly April.

J	F	M	A	M	J	J	A	S	O	N	D
		7	3	1	*	3					

Swift *Apus apus*
Very common Spring passage migrant and Summer visitor. Early arrival second week March, main passage end of March to mid-May. Autumn passage lighter. September to early November.

Pallid Swift *Apus pallidus*
Scarce passage migrant and Summer visitor. Passage early April and mid September.

Alpine Swift *Apus melba*
Common passage migrant and Summer visitor. Spring mid March-early May peaks during latter half April. Autumn first half of October. Present 20 March-24 October. Highest count (100+ 8 October 1992).

White-breasted Kingfisher *Halcyon smyrnensis*
Vagrant 1 record August 9th 1989. [N. Curry]

Common Kingfisher *Alcedo atthis*
Passage migrant and winter visitor. Autumn passage August-October.

Blue-cheeked Bee-eater *Merops superciliosus*
Vagrant 4+ records.
1987 1 Hersonissos 6.4. (W T Appleyard).
1988 1 on south coast below Komatides, nr.Chora Sfakion in olive grove 27.4.(J. Steele & Dr. K. Steele) photographed.
1990 1 photographed at Tymbaki 6.4. (Juilliard et. al, 1990).
1991 1 21st April 1991 2 miles north of Elaphonisi. (A. Henderson, P. Evans, M.Gold).
1992 1 near Xerokampos 18.4. (M. Leuenberger).

Bee-eater *Merops apiaster*
Regular passage migrant in Spring. Early April to third week of May.
Very common some years. Fewer in Autumn, September to early October.

J	F	M	A	M	J	J	A	S	O	N	D
		◆	◆					◆	◆		

Roller *Coracias garrulus*
Vagrant/Very Rare passage migrant. April-May and August.

J	F	M	A	M	J	J	A	S	O	N	D
		5	8				3	2			

Hoopoe *Upupa epops*
Regular passage migrant in Spring. March-early May.
Very small numbers August - October.

J	F	M	A	M	J	J	A	S	O	N	D
		28	100+	18			3	20+	3		

Wryneck *Jynx torquilla*
Scarce passage migrant during April. Rare in Autumn October.

J	F	M	A	M	J	J	A	S	O	N	D
		1	27	*	2			8			
								6			

Dupont's Lark *Chersophilus duponti*
Vagrant. One record Damnoni beach 16.4.88.(D.Ireland, J.Osborne, RSPB tour)

Calandra Lark *Melanocorypha calandra*
Rare passage migrant April-May, October

Short-toed Lark *Calandrella brachydactyla*
Passage migrant late March-early May, main passage in April. Autumn, August to September. Winter visitor October to February. A few pairs may breed.

J	F	M	A	M	J	J	A	S	O	N	D
◆	◆	◆	◆	◆	◆		◆	◆	◆	◆	◆

Crested Lark *Galerida cristata*
Common resident

Woodlark *Lullula arborea*
Frequent resident, and passage migrant, April.

Skylark *Alauda arvensis*
Winter visitor October- end of March. A few pairs may breed.

Sand Martin *Riparia riparia*
Summer visitor. Common passage migrant mid March to mid May. Peak April. Autumn small peaks Sept/October.

Crag Martin *Ptyonoprogne rupestris*
Common resident, movement to lowlands in Winter and passage migrant mid February.

Swallow *Hirundo rustica*
Common summer visitor and passage migrant. Spring passage mid-March to mid May peak second half April. Autumn passage, September to November.

Red-rumped Swallow *Hirundo daurica*
Spring passage migrant and regularly but scarce summer visitor. March-Sept. Passage late March-early May, peak April. Occasional December records.

House Martin *Delichon urbica*
Common Spring passage migrant mid March-May. Peak early May. Summer visitor in small numbers. March-Sept. Scarce in Autumn.

Richard's Pipit *Anthus novaeseelandiae*
Vagrant, only 3 records October 1987, April 1989 and May 1992, 3 birds.

Tawny Pipit *Anthus campestris*
Frequent Spring passage migrant March-May, peak April. Scarce Summer visitor. Rare in Autumn August - October. One December 1992.

J	F	M	A	M	J	J	A	S	O	N	D
		23	142	43			66	12	23		1

Tree Pipit *Anthus trivialis*
Common Spring passage migrant late April-early May.
Peak 3rd week April. Scarce in Autumn, a few may Winter

J	F	M	A	M	J	J	A	S	O	N	D
◆	◆	◆					◆			◆	◆

Meadow Pipit *Anthus pratensis*
Common Winter visitor mid October-April.

Red-throated Pipit *Anthus cervinus*
Frequent Spring passage migrant end of March-first week in May. Scarce in Autumn, October - November.

Water Pipit *Anthus spinoletta*
Very Rare Spring and Autumn Passage migrant.

J	F	M	A	M	J	J	A	S	O	N	D
		3	3	2					3		

Yellow Wagtail *Motacilla (flava) flavissima*
Common Spring passage migrant, mid March-early May, peaks April. Autumn small numbers August-October.

Grey Wagtail *Motacilla cinerea*
Regular Winter visitor, October-April.

J	F	M	A	M	J	J	A	S	O	N	D
17	14	◆	6	1				1	42	12	11

White Wagtail *Motacilla alba*
Resident, Common winter visitor, evidence of Spring passage early April. *Motacilla a. yarrelli* possibly rare passage migrant March-May.

Wren *Troglodytes troglodytes*
Frequent resident, most records from upland areas and gorges.

Dunnock *Prunella modularis*
Vagrant or Rare winter visitor, only two records, single birds March and April 1987.

Alpine Accentor *Prunella collaris*
Rare resident, records only from Mt Psiloritis, White Mountains and Kourtaliotiko Gorge. Probably under recorded.

Rufous Bush Chat *Cercotrichas galactotes*
Vagrant, only single records April and May 1986, but several records 1993.
1993 1 Akrotiri Stavros 14.4. (RD Wilson).
    1 Samaria Gorge 24.4. (J&J Day).
    4 Imbros Gorge 27.4. (J&J Day).
    1 Falasarna 2.5.(J&J Day).

Robin *Erithacus rubecula*
Common winter visitor October-March.

Thrush Nightingale *Luscinia luscinia*
Very rare passage migrant. April/May.

Nightingale *Luscinia megarhynchos*
Regular passage migrant April-mid May.

J	F	M	A	M	J	J	A	S	O	N	D
		♦	♦	♦	♦						

Black Redstart *Phoenicurus ochruros*
Common winter visitor October-March, few April.

Common Redstart *Phoenicurus phoenicurus*
Regular passage migrant in small numbers, main peak April; fewer in Autumn, mainly October.

J	F	M	A	M	J	J	A	S	O	N	D
		2	99	6	2			12	24	1	

Whinchat *Saxicola rubetra*
Common passage migrant, A few birds summer.
Spring late March-May, peaks April.
Autumn late September-October. Fewer than Spring.

J	F	M	A	M	J	J	A	S	O	N	D
♦		♦	♦	♦	♦	♦	♦	♦		♦	

Stonechat *Saxicola torquata*
Common and widespread resident.

Isabelline Wheatear *Oenanthe isabellina*
Scarce passage migrant mainly late March-April.

J	F	M	A	M	J	J	A	S	O	N	D
		15	20	1			1		1		

Wheatear *Oenanthe oenanthe*
Common passage migrant mid March-early May peaks April. Fewer in Autumn, August-October, singles early November. Summer visitor in fewer numbers.

J	F	M	A	M	J	J	A	S	O	N	D
	◆	◆	◆	◆	◆	◆	◆	◆	◆	◆	

Black-eared Wheatear *Oenanthe hispanica*
Common summer visitor and Spring passage migrant, mid-March to May, peaks during April and May. Fewer in Autumn.

J	F	M	A	M	J	J	A	S	O	N	D
	◆	◆	◆	◆			◆	◆			

White-crowned Black Wheatear *Oenanthe leucopyga*
1993 15.4.1993 1 male photographed at the side of the road between Lakki and Omalos. (Joan Potts and High Peak RSPB group).

Rock Thrush *Monticola saxatilis*
Vagrant, only five records April and August

Blue Rock Thrush *Monticola solitarius*
Common resident, widespread.

Ring Ouzel *Turdus torquatus*
Vagrant, only three records 1986-1992.

J	F	M	A	M	J	J	A	S	O	N	D
			1	1					1		

1986 1 Falasarna 12.5. (J.Owen et al).
1987 1 Knossos 8.4. (J.Adams et al).
1989 1 Malia between 20.10. & 26.10. (Margot Lidstone, Nicola Duckworth).

Blackbird *Turdus merula*
Common resident. Winter visitor October-March.

Fieldfare *Turdus pilaris*
Winter vagrant.
1989 Up to 3 Malia 24-26 March 1989.(G.Clark).

Song Thrush *Turdus philomelos*
Common Winter visitor. October-March.

Mistle Thrush *Turdus viscivorus*
Regular Winter visitor. October-March.

J	Г	M	A	M	J	J	A	S	O	N	D
◆	◆	6							1	1	*

Cetti's Warbler *Cettia cetti*
Common resident, widepread.

Fan-tailed Warbler *Cisticola juncidis*
Resident recorded regularly at approx. 26 sites. - April-July.(C&JH).

Grasshopper Warbler *Locustella naevia*
Very rare passage migrant, only three records

J	F	M	A	M	J	J	A	S	O	N	D
		2	1								

Savi's Warbler *Locustella luscinioides*
Very rare passage migrant.

J	F	M	A	M	J	J	A	S	O	N	D
		4							1		

Moustached Warbler *Acrocephalus melanopogon*
Scarce but regular Spring passage migrant, late March-early May. 1 record October 1994

Aquatic Warbler *Acrocephalus paludicola*
Vagrant 2 records. 1994 1 Agia 5.94. (J. S. Mighell) Record pending.
1 Agia 22.10.94. (P. J. Wilson) Record pending.

Sedge Warbler *Acrocephalus schoenobaenus*
Common Spring passage migrant Feb, late March-early May. Scarce summmmer visitor August. Autumn passage September

Marsh Warbler *Acrocephalus palustris*
Very rare passage migrant mid April-early June.

Reed Warbler *Acrocephalus scirpaceus*
Regular Spring passage migrant late March-early May, peak April. Summer visitor in small numbers, a few winter.

Great Reed Warbler *Acrocephalus arundinaceus*
Frequent Spring passage migrant April-early May.
Perhaps scarce summer visitor. Autumn passage: August, September.

Olivaceous Warbler *Hippolais pallida*
Scarce but regular passage migrant April and October. Summer visitor in small numbers arriving mid May. Probably underrecorded.

Olive-tree Warbler *Hippolais olivetorum*
Very Rare passage migrant April-May. August-September.

Icterine Warbler *Hippolais icterina*
Scarce passage migrant April-May. August-September.

Marmora's Warbler *Sylvia sarda*
Vagrant, only three records. 1 May, 2 between Georgioupolis and Lake Kournas 4. & 6. 10. 1989 [M.Slater]
1989 1 male Arkadi 10.5. (P. Marriott)

Spectacled Warbler *Sylvia conspicillata*
Vagrant only two records April 1989, and April 1991
1989 12.4. Moni Prevelli (C.Hind)
1991 3.4. 1 male near Rethymnon harbour (D. Townsend).

70

Subalpine Warbler *Sylvia cantillans*
Frequent Spring passage migrant, April. Male dead at side of road with brood patches near Rethymnon 1991. Pair at Elafonisi 20.4. 1995.

J	F	M	A	M	J	J	A	S	O	N	D
	◆	◆	◆	◆					◆		

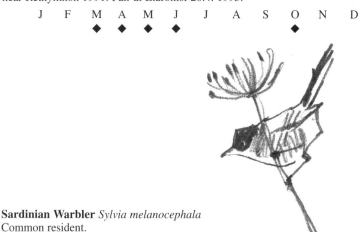

Sardinian Warbler *Sylvia melanocephala*
Common resident.

Rüppell's Warbler *Sylvia rueppelli*
Regular passage migrant late March-mid April. Scarce but widespread Summer visitor. Return passage in October.

Orphean Warbler *Sylvia hortensis*
Rare passage migrant, April, September-October.

Barred Warbler *Sylvia nisoria*
Vagrant, only two records April and October 1989.
1989 1 Moni Prevelli 14.4.(DT Ireland, J.Osborne et al)
1989 1 Chania October 1989 (D.M. Morrison)

Lesser Whitethroat *Sylvia curraca*
Rare passage migrant, April, August, September, October.

Common Whitethroat *Sylvia communis*
Regular Spring passage migrant. April-early May.
Scarce Autumn, September-November. A few may breed.

Garden Warbler *Sylvia borin*
Scarce Spring migrant, April-early May. One record November.

J	F	M	A	M	J	J	A	S	O	N	D
		15	13			1			1		

Blackcap *Sylvia atricapilla*
Regular Spring passage migrant, late March-early May, peak April. Autumn rare October and November.

Bonelli's Warbler *Phylloscopus bonelli*
Very scarce Spring passage migrant mainly April. 1 record May. Two October records.

Wood Warbler *Phylloscopus sibilatrix*
Frequent Spring passage migrant April-early May, peaks mid April.
Autumn scarce, September-early November.

Chiffchaff *Phylloscopus collybita*
Common Winter visitor late November-March
Frequent passage migrant March-early April and September-October.

Willow Warbler *Phylloscopus trochilus*
Frequent passage migrant. Spring: Late March. April
Autumn, mid September to third week October.

Goldcrest *Regulus regulus*
Very rare passage migrant and Winter visitor

J	F	M	A	M	J	J	A	S	O	N	D
	2		5	2					5		

Firecrest *Regulus ignicapillus*
Very rare resident. Rare passage migrant May.
Five records only all May and 1 record April 1993 near Agios Pandos 23.4. (J&J Day).

Spotted Flycatcher *Muscicapa striata*
Common passage migrant second week April-second week May.
Autumn passage early August-third week in October. One winter record January 1992.
Regular Summer visitor.

Red-breasted Flycatcher *Ficedula parva*
Very rare passage migrant

J	F	M	A	M	J	J	A	S	O	N	D
			3					4	1		

Semi-collared Flycatcher *Ficedula semitorquata*
Vagrant.

J	F	M	A	M	J	J	A	S	O	N	D
			2					1		1	

Collared Flycatcher *Ficedula albicollis*
Frequent Spring passage migrant, April-early-mid May.
1994 ¬ 3rd week in May.

Pied Flycatcher *Ficedula hypoleuca*
Frequent Spring Passage migrant, April-mid May. Autumn records Sept.

Coal Tit *Parus ater*
Rare resident

Blue Tit *Parus caeruleus*
Common resident

Great Tit *Parus major*
Common resident

Rock Nuthatch *Sitta neumayer*
Very rare resident. One record October 1989.
1989 1 during one date in the first half of October. (DM Morrison).

Short-toed Treecreeper *Certhia brachydactyla*
Rare resident, only recorded in mountains and gorges. Westwards from Plakias to Paleochora. Most frequent Samaria Gorge, Imbros Gorge and Ag.Irini Gorge.

Penduline Tit *Remiz pendulinus*
Scarce resident increasing from 1986. Small flocks in 1992.

J	F	M	A	M	J	J	A	S	O	N	D
◆	◆	◆	◆	◆						◆	◆

Golden Oriole *Oriolus oriolus*
Regular Spring passage migrant April- mid May. Peak late April- early May. Scarce in Autumn, September. Rare Summer Visitor.

Isabelline Shrike *Lanius isabellinus*
Vagrant two records,
1988 4.10. (C.Hind)
1991 17.5. (S.Foster)

Red-backed Shrike *Lanius collurio*
Rare Spring passage migrant.
Regular Autumn mid August-October. Peak September.
Late record 2 27th November 1990. (C&JH).

Lesser Grey Shrike *Lanius minor*
Rare Spring passage migrant April - May. Autumn, scarce mainly August.

Woodchat Shrike *Lanius senator*
Regular Passage migrant mid-March-April.
Scarce summer visitor, evidence of Autumn passage during August and Sept.

Masked Shrike *Lanius nubicus*
Very rare passage migrant. April-May.

Jay *Garrulus glandarius*
Resident and frequent

Alpine Chough *Pyrrhocorax graculus*
Scarce resident mainly mountains and gorges Lassithi-Samaria & Monasteraki.

Chough *Pyrrhocorax pyrrhocorax*
Resident. Frequent in gorges and mountains. Winter roosts in Monasteraki. Flocks of 20-100. Recorded every month.

Jackdaw *Corvus monedula*
Common resident.

Hooded Crow *Corvus cornix*
Common resident, widespread

Common Raven *Corvus corax*
Common resident

Common Starling *Sturnus vulgaris*
Common Winter visitor, October to March.

House Sparrow *Passer domesticus*
Common resident. *P.d.italiae* outnumbers *P. domesticus*

Spanish Sparrow *Passer hispaniolensis*
Frequent resident and passage migrant April.

Tree Sparrow *Passer montanus*
Frequent resident.

Rock Sparrow *Petronia petronia*
Vagrant, only two records.
1990 1 opposite Rethymna Beach Hotel 24.10.90. (Marjorie & Stewart Hall)
1995 1 Prevelli Bridge 9.4.(C&JH). Records pending).

Chaffinch *Fringilla coelebs*
Widespread and abundant resident.

Serin *Serinus serinus*
Frequent resident.

J	F	M	A	M	J	J	A	S	O	N	D
21	2	27	79	31	8			5	20	1	9

Greenfinch *Carduelis chloris*
Common Resident and winter visitor. October-March

Goldfinch *Carduelis carduelis*
Common resident and winter visitor, October-March.

Siskin *Carduelis spinus*
Scarce winter visitor October-March.

Linnet *Carduelis cannabina*
Frequent resident and winter visitor. September-early April.

Common Crossbill *Loxia curvirostra*
Resident in very small numbers, not recorded before 1989.

J	F	M	A	M	J	J	A	S	O	N	D
	5	3	2			1			20		

Common Rosefinch *Carpodacus erythrinus.*
1994 1 record a male Aposelemis river 12.9.(C&JH).

Hawfinch Coccothraustes coccothraustes
Very rare passage migrant April.

Cirl Bunting *Emberiza cirlus*
Fairly common resident

Rock Bunting *Emberiza cia*
Very rare resident, or Accidental visitor April & October.

Ortolan Bunting *Emberiza hortulana*
Spring Passage migrant in small numbers April-early May.
Scarce Summer visitor.

Cretzschmar's Bunting *Emberiza caesia*
Very rare passage migrant April and May.

Reed Bunting *Emberiza schoeniclus*
Very rare winter visitor, passage migrant. Only records April and October. & Jan, Feb, & March.

Black-headed Bunting *Emberiza melanocephala*
Very Rare passage migrant, first week in May.

Corn Bunting *Miliaria calandra*
Common resident and Winter visitor.

BIBLIOGRAPHY AND RECOMMENDED BOOKS.

General
Cameron Pat. Blue Guide to Crete. 6th Edit. Black/Norton.
Bowman John. The Travellers' Guides. Crete Jonathan Cape.
Rough Guide to Crete. Harrap, Columbus.

Walking Books
Godfrey, Karslake. Landscapes of Eastern Crete. Sunflower Books.
Godfrey, Karslake. Landscapes of Western Crete. Sunflower Books.
Caughey, B & N. Crete off the Beaten Track. Cicerone.

Flowers
Huxley and Taylor. Flowers of Greece and the Aegean, Chatto and Windus
Turland, Chilton & Press. Flora of the Cretan Area. Annotated Checklist and Atlas.
HMSO
Blamey/Grey-Wilson Mediterranean Wild Flowers. Harper Collins
Polunin O. Guide to Flowers of Greece and the Balkans. Oxford
Vedel. Trees and Shrubs of the Mediterranean. Out of print, Penguin

Birds
Heinzel, Fitter and Parslow. The Birds of Britain and Europe. Collins
Gensbol. The Birds of Prey of Britain and Europe, North Africa and the Middle East.
Collins
Porter et al. Flight Identification of European Raptors. Poyser.
Jonsson. Birds of Europe. Helm.
Jonsson. Birds of the Mediterranean and Alps. Croom Helm. Out of print.
Handrinos, Demetropoulos. Birds of Prey of Greece. Efstathiadis Group

Animals
Corbet and (Ovenden) The Mammals of Great Britain and Europe. Collins 1980.
Schober and Grimmberger. Bats of Britain and Europe. Hamlyn 1993. (Ovenden).
A Field Guide to the Reptiles and Amphibians of Great Britain and Europe. Collins 1978.

Insects
Higgins and Riley. Butterflies of Britain and Europe. Collins 1970.
Whalley. Butterflies. Mitchell Beazley 1981.
Chinery. Insects of Britain and Western Europe. Collins 1986.

BIBLIOGRAPHY

Lambert A. A specific checklist of the birds of Crete. Ibis 99: 43-68 1957
Aberdeen University Crete Expedition 1974. Crete Ringing Report 1973-1975.
Vallianos C. Les oiseaux observés en Crète Biologia Gallo-Hellenica, Vol.11,1,pp 111-127,1984
Swann and Baillie. Bird Study 26; 55-58 March 1979.
The suspension of moult by trans-Saharan migrants in Crete.
Cramp. Handbook of the Birds of Western Palearctic. Vols 1-9
Bottleneck areas for Migratory Birds in the Mediterranean Region. ICBP Study report 18.
Vagliano C 1985. NP
The continental and island migration route of the south east Mediterranean: problems and

propositions. In: Newton and Chancellor R.D. Conservation studies on raptors. ICBP Technical Pub. No 5 pp 263-269.
Crete Reports 1986-1994. Compiled by Coghlan, Johnson and Townsend.
Parrott J., Gooders and Coghlan. BOU Checklist for the Birds of Crete. (in prep.)

RECORDS:
Please submit records of rare and vagrant birds to the recorder for Greece, George Handrinos, 44 El. Venizelou Str., 166 75, Glyfada, Greece.
Further records and comments on this 4th edition to:
Stephanie Coghlan, 25 Thorpe Lane, Almondbury, Huddersfield, West Yorks HD5 8TA.

ANNUAL REPORTS
Annual reports have been compiled from records for the years 1986-1994.
Copies of these are available from the above address.

GUIDING ON CRETE:
Contact John and Chris Henshall for details. Their address is: Kalo Horio, Pediados, Heraklion, GR 700 14, Limni Hersonison, Crete, Greece.
   Tel: 30 (0) 897 41980
   Fax: 30 (0) 81 223357

Woodlark

Key to symbols:

RB = Resident Breeder   MB = Migrant Breeder   OB = Occasional Breeder

PM = Passage Migrant   WV = Winter Visitor   AV = Accidental Visitor

BIRDS

Status	English name	Scientific name							
PM, RB, WV	Little Grebe	*Tachybaptus ruficollis*							
PM, WV	Great Crested Grebe	*Podiceps cristatus*							
PM, WV	Black-necked Grebe	*Podiceps nigricollis*							
PM, MB	Cory's Shearwater	*Calonectris diomedea*							
PM, MB	Med. Shearwater	*Puffinus yelkouan*							
PM, VV	Cormorant	*Phalacrocorax carbo*							
RB	Shag	*Phalacrocorax aristotelis*							
AV	Pygmy Cormorant	*Phalacrocrax pygmeus*							
AV	White Pelican	*Pelecanus onocrotalus*							
AV	Dalmatian Pelican	*Pelecanus crispus*							
PM	Bittern	*Botaurus stellaris*							
PM	Little Bittern	*Ixobrychus minutus*							
PM	Night Heron	*Nycticorax nycticorax*							
PM	Squacco Heron	*Ardeola ralloides*							
AV	Cattle Egret	*Bubulcus ibis*							
PM	Little Egret	*Egretta garzetta*							
PM	Great White Egret	*Egretta alba*							
PM	Grey Heron	*Ardea cinerea*							
PM	Purple Heron	*Ardea purpurea*							
PM, AV	Black Stork	*Ciconia nigra*							
PM	White Stork	*Ciconia ciconia*							
PM	Glossy Ibis	*Plegadis falcinellus*							
PM	Spoonbill	*Platalea leucorodia*							
PM	Greater Flamingo	*Phoenicopterus ruber*							
AV	Mute Swan	*Cygnus olor*							
AV	Shelduck	*Tadorna tadorna*							
PM, WV	Wigeon	*Anas penelope*							
PM, WV	Gadwall	*Anas strepera*							
PM, WV	Teal	*Anas crecca*							
PM, RB, WV	Mallard	*Anas platyrhynchos*							
PM, WV	Pintail	*Anas acuta*							
PM, RB?	Garganey	*Anas querquedula*							
PM, WV	Shoveler	*Anas clypeata*							
PM, AV	Marbled Teal	*Marmaronetta angustirostris*							
AV	Red-crested Pochard	*Netta rufina*							
PM, RB?, WV	Pochard	*Aythya ferina*							
PM, RB, WV	Ferruginous Duck	*Aythya nyroca*							
PM, WV	Tufted Duck	*Aythya fuligula*							
AV	Red-breasted Merganser	*Mergus serrator*							
PM	Honey Buzzard	*Pernis apivorus*							
PM	Black Kite	*Milvus migrans*							
PM	Red Kite	*Milvus milvus*							
RB	Lammergeier	*Gypaetus barbatus*							
PM	Egyptian Vulture	*Neophron percnopterus*							

Status	English name	Scientific name						
RB	Griffon Vulture	*Gyps fulvus*						
AV	Black Vulture	*Aegypius monachus*						
PM	Short-toed Eagle	*Circaetus gallicus*						
PM, MB?, WV	Marsh Harrier	*Circus aeruginosus*						
PM, WV	Hen Harrier	*Circus cyaneus*						
PM	Pallid Harrier	*Circus macrourus*						
PM	Montagu's Harrier	*Circus pygargus*						
PM, WV	Goshawk	*Accipter gentilis*						
PM, WV	Sparrowhawk	*Accipter nisus*						
RB?, AV	Levant Sparrowhawk	*Accipter brevipes*						
PM, RB, WV	Buzzard	*Buteo buteo*						
PM, RB?	Long-legged Buzzard	*Buteo rufinus*						
AV	Lesser Spotted Eagle	*Aquila pomarina*						
AV	Spotted Eagle	*Aquila clanga*						
AV	Tawny/Steppe Eagle	*Aquila rapax*						
RB	Golden Eagle	*Aquila chrysaetos*						
PM, WV	Botted Eagle	*Hieraaetus pennatus*						
RB	Bonellis Eagle	*Hieraaetus fasciatus*						
PM	Osprey	*Pandion haliaetus*						
PM, RB?	Lesser Kestrel	*Falco naumanni*						
PM, RB, WV	Kestrel	*Falco tinnunculus*						
PM	Red-footed Falcon	*Falco vespertinus*						
PM, WV	Merlin	*Falco columbarius*						
PM, OB?	Hobby	*Falco subbuteo*						
PM, RB?	Lanner	*Falco biarmicus*						
PM, MB	Eleonoras Falcon	*Falco eleonorae*						
PM, RB, WV	Peregrine	*Falco peregrinus*						
RB	Chukar	*Alectoris chukar*						
PM, MB, WV?	Quail	*Coturnix coturnix*						
PM, WV	Water Rail	*Rallus aquaticus*						
PM	Spotted Crake	*Porzana porzana*						
PM	Little Crake	*Porzana parva*						
PM	Baillons Crake	*Porzana pusilla*						
AV	Corncrake	*Crex crex*						
PM, RB, WV	Moorhen	*Gallinula chloropus*						
PM, RB? WV	Coot	*Fulica atra*						
PM	Crane	*Grus grus*						
PM, AV	Oystercatcher	*Haematopus ostralegus*						
PM	Black-winged Stilt	*Himantopus himantopus*						
PM, AV	Avocet	*Recurvirostra avosetta*						
PM, MB, WV	Stone Curlew	*Burhinus oedicnemus*						
AV	Cream-coloured Courser	*Cursorius cursor*						
PM	Collared Pratincole	*Glareola pratincola*						
AV	Black-winged Pratincole	*Glareola nordmanni*						
PM, MB	Little Ringed Plover	*Charadrius dubius*						
PM, WV	Ringed Plover	*Charadrius hiaticula*						
PM, WV	Kentish Plover	*Charadrius alexandrinus*						
AV	Greater Sand Plover	*C. leschenaultii*						
AV	Caspian Plover	*C. asiaticus*						
AV	Dotterel	*C. morinellus*						
PM, WV	Golden Plover	*Pluvialis apricaria*						

Status	English name	Scientific name						
AV	Pacific Golden Plover	*Pluvialis fulva*						
PM	Grey Plover	*Pluvialis squatarola*						
AV	Spur-winged Plover	*Hoplopterus spinosus*						
AV	Sociable Plover	*Chettusia gregaria*						
AV	White-tailed Plover	*Chettusia leucura*						
WV	Lapwing	*Vanellus vanellus*						
AV	Knot	*Calidris canutus*						
PM	Sanderling	*Calidris alba*						
PM	Little Stint	*Calidris minuta*						
PM	Temmincks Stint	*Calidris temminckii*						
PM	Curlew Sandpiper	*Calidris ferruginea*						
PM	Dunlin	*Calidris alpina*						
PM	Ruff	*Philomachus pugnax*						
PM	Jack Snipe	*Lymnocryptes minimus*						
AV	Snipe	*Gallinago gallinago*						
PM, WV	Great Snipe	*Gallinago media*						
PM, WV	Woodcock	*Scolopax rusticola*						
PM	Black-tailed Godwit	*Limosa limosa*						
PM, WV	Whimbrel	*Numenius phaeopus*						
PM, WV	Curlew	*Numenius arquata*						
PM	Spotted Redshank	*Tringa erythropus*						
PM, WV	Redshank	*Tringa totanus*						
PM	Marsh Sandpiper	*Tringa stagnatilis*						
PM	Greenshank	*Tringa nebularia*						
PM, WV?	Green Sandpiper	*Tringa ochropus*						
PM	Wood Sandpiper	*Tringa glareola*						
PM, WV	Common Sandpiper	*Actitis hypoleucos*						
PM	Turnstone	*Arenaria interpres*						
WV	Great Black-headed Gull	*Larus ichthyaetus*						
PM, WV	Mediterranean Gull	*Larus melanocephalus*						
PM	Little Gull	*Larus minutus*						
PM, WV	Black-headed Gull	*Larus ridibundus*						
AV	Slender-billed Gull	*Larus genei*						
RB	Audouin's Gull	*Larus audouinii*						
PM, AV	Common Gull	*Larus canus*						
PM, WV	Lesser Black-backed Gull	*Larus fuscus*						
RB	Yellow-legged Herring Gull	*Larus c. michahellis*						
AV	Kittiwake	*Rissa tridactyla*						
PM	Gull-billed Tern	*Gelochelidon nilotica*						
PM	Caspian Tern	*Sterna caspia*						
PM, WV	Sandwich Tern	*Sterna sandvicensis*						
PM	Common Tern	*Sterna hirundo*						
PM	Little Tern	*Sterna albifrons*						
PM	Whiskered Tern	*Chlidonias hybridus*						
PM	Black Tern	*Chlidonias niger*						
PM	White-winged Black Tern	*Chlidonias leucopterus*						
PM	Rock Dove	*Columba livia*						
OB?	Stock Dove	*Columba oenas*						
PM?, RB, WV?	Wood Pigeon	*Columba palumbus*						
RB	Collared Dove	*Streptopelia decaocto*						
PM, MB	Turtle Dove	*Streptopelia turtur*						

Status	English name	Scientific name						
PM, GR	Spotted Cuckoo	*Clamator glandarius*						
PM	Cuckoo	*Cuculus canorus*						
RM, WV?	Barn Owl	*Tyto alba*						
RB, MB	Scops Owl	*Otus scops*						
RB	Little Owl	*Athene noctua*						
PM, RB?	Long-eared Owl	*Asio otus*						
PM, WV	Short-eared Owl	*Asio flammeus*						
PM, MB	Nightjar	*Caprimulgus europaeus*						
PM, MB	Swift	*Apus apus*						
PM, MB	Pallio Swift	*Apus pallidus*						
PM, MB	Alpine Swift	*Apus melba*						
PM, RB, WV	Kingfisher	*Alcedo atthis*						
AV	Blue-cheeked Bee-eater	*Merops superciliosus*						
PM	Bee-eater	*Merops apiaster*						
PM	Roller	*Coracias garrulus*						
PM	Hoopoe	*Upupa epops*						
PM	Wryneck	*Jynx torquilla*						
AV	Dupont's Lark	*Chersophilus duponti*						
PM	Calandra Lark	*Melanocorypha calandra*						
PM, MB, WV	Short-toed Lark	*Calandrella brachydactyla*						
PM, RB	Crested Lark	*Galerida cristata*						
PM, RB	Woodlark	*Lullula arborea*						
PM, WV	Skylark	*Alauda arvensis*						
PM	Sand Martin	*Riparia riparia*						
PM?, RB	Crag Martin	*Ptyonoprogne rupestris*						
PM, MB	Swallow	*Hirundo rustica*						
PM, MB	Red-rumped Swallow	*Hirundo daurica*						
PM, MB	House Martin	*Delichon urbica*						
PM	Richard's Pipit	*Anthus novaeseelandiae*						
PM, MB?	Tawny Pipit	*Anthus campestris*						
PM	Tree Pipit	*Anthus trivialis*						
PM, OB?, WV	Meadow Pipit	*Anthus pratensis*						
PM	Red-throated Pipit	*Anthus cervinus*						
PM, WV	Water Pipit	*Anthus spinoletta*						
PM, OB	Yellow Wagtail	*Motacilla flava*						
PM, OB, WV	Grey Wagtail	*Motacilla cinerea*						
PM, RB, WV	White Wagtail	*Motacilla alba*						
RB, WV	Wren	*Troglodytes troglodytes*						
WV	Dunnock	*Prunella modularis*						
RB	Alpine Accentor	*Prunella collaris*						
PM, AV	Rufus Bush Chat	*Cercotrichas galactotes*						
PM, WV	Robin	*Erithacus rubecula*						
PM	Thrush Nightingale	*Luscinia luscinia*						
PM, MB	Nightingale	*Luscinia megarhynchos*						
PM, WV	Bluethroat	*Luscinia svecica*						
PM, WV	Black Redstart	*Phoenicurus ochrurus*						
PM	Redstart	*Phoenicurus phoenicurus*						
PM, OB?	Whinchat	*Saxicola rubetra*						
PM, RB, WV	Stonechat	*Saxicola torquata*						
PM, OB	Isabelline Wheatear	*Oenanthe isabellina*						
PM, MB	Wheatear	*Oenanthe oenanthe*						

Status	English name	Scientific name							
PM, MB	Black-eared Wheatear	*Oenanthe hispanica*							
AV	White-crowned Blk Wheatear	*O. leucopyga*							
PM	Rock Thrush	*Monticola saxitilis*							
PM, RB, WV	Blue Rock Thrush	*Monticola solitarius*							
PM	Ring Ouzel	*Turdus torquatus*							
PM, RB, WV	Blackbird	*Turdus merula*							
PM, WV	Song Thrush	*Turdus philomelos*							
WV	Mistle Thrush	*Turdus viscivorus*							
RB	Cetti's Warbler	*Cettia cetti*							
RB	Fan-tailed Warbler	*Cisticola juncidis*							
PM	Grasshopper Warbler	*Locustella naevia*							
PM	Savi's Warbler	*Locustella lusciniodes*							
PM, WV	Moustached Warbler	*Acrocephalus melanopogon*							
AV	Aquatic Warbler	*Acrocephalus paludicola*							
PM	Sedge Warbler	*Acrocephalus schoenobaenus*							
PM	Marsh Warbler	*Acrocephalus palustris*							
PM	Reed Warbler	*Acrocephalus scirpaceus*							
PM, MB	Great Reed Warbler	*Acrocephalus arundinaceus*							
PM, MB	Olivaceous Warbler	*Hippolais pallida*							
PM, MB?	Olivetree Warbler	*Hippolais olivetorum*							
PM	Icterine Warbler	*Hippolais icterina*							
RB?, AV?	Marmoras Warbler	*Sylvia sarda*							
AV	Spectacled Warbler	*Sylvia conspicillata*							
PM, MB	Subalpine Warbler	*Sylvia cantillans*							
PM, RB, WV?	Sardinian Warbler	*Sylvia melanocephala*							
PM, MB	Ruppell's Warbler	*Sylvia rüppelli*							
PM, MB	Orphean Warbler	*Sylvia hortensis*							
PM	Barred Warbler	*Sylvia nisoria*							
PM	Lesser Whitethroat	*Sylvia curruca*							
PM, MB	Whitethroat	*Sylvia communis*							
PM	Garden Warbler	*Sylvia borin*							
PM, WV	Blackcap	*Sylvia atricapilla*							
PM	Bonelli's Warbler	*Phylloscopus bonelli*							
PM, WV	Wood Warbler	*Phylloscopus sibilatrix*							
PM, WV	Chiffchaff	*Phylloscopus collybita*							
PM	Willow Warbler	*Phylloscopus trochilus*							
RB?, WV	Goldcrest	*Regulus regulus*							
MB, WV	Firecrest	*Regulus ignicapillus*							
PM, MB	Spotted Flycatcher	*Muscicapa striata*							
PM	Red-breasted Flycatcher	*Ficedula parva*							
PM	Collared Flycatcher	*Ficedula albicollis*							
PM	Pied Flycatcher	*Ficedula hypoleuca*							
RB?	Sombre Tit	*Parus lugubris*							
RB?	Coal Tit	*Parus ater*							
RB	Blue Tit	*Parus caeruleus*							
RB	Great Tit	*Parus major*							
AV	Rock Nuthatch	*Sitta neumayer*							
RB	Short-toed Treecreeper	*Certhia brachydactyla*							
RB, WV	Penduline Tit	*Remiz pendulinus*							
PM	Golden Oriole	*Oriolus oriolus*							
AV	Isabelline Shrike	*Lanius isabellinus*							

Status	English name	Scientific name						
PM	Red-backed Shrike	*Lanius collurio*						
PM	Lesser Grey Shrike	*Lanius minor*						
PM, MB	Woodchat Shrike	*Lanius senator*						
AV	Masked Shrike	*Lanius nubicus*						
RB	Jay	*Garrulus glandarius*						
RB	Alpine Chough	*Pyrrhocorax graculus*						
RB	Chough	*Pyrrhocorax pyrrhocorax*						
RB	Jackdaw	*Corvus monedula*						
RB	Hooded Crow	*Corvus corone cornix*						
RB	Raven	*Corvus corax*						
PM, WV	Starling	*Sturnus vulgaris*						
RB	House Sparrow	*Passer domesticus*						
RB	Italian Sparrow	*Passer domesticus italiae*						
PM, WV	Spanish Sparrow	*Passer hispaniolensis*						
PM, WV	Tree Sparrow	*Passer montanus*						
AV	Rock Sparrow	*Petronia petronia*						
PM, RB, WV	Chaffinch	*Fringilla coelebs*						
WV	Brambling	*Fringilla montifringilla*						
PM, RB, WV	Serin	*Serinus serinus*						
PM, RB, WV	Greenfinch	*Carduelis chloris*						
PM, RB, WV	Goldfinch	*Carduelis carduelis*						
PM, WV	Siskin	*Carduelis spinus*						
PM, RB, WV	Linnet	*Carduelis cannabina*						
OB?, WV	Crossbill	*Loxia curvirostra*						
AV	Trumpeter Finch	*Bucanetes githagineus*						
PM, WV	Hawfinch	*Coccothraustes coccothraustes*						
RB	Cirl Bunting	*Emberiza cirlus*						
AV	Rock Bunting	*Emberiza cia*						
PM, MB	Ortolan	*Emberiza hortulana*						
PM	Cretzschmar's Bunting	*Emberiza caesia*						
WV	Reed Bunting	*Emberiza schoeniclus*						
PM, MB	Black-headed Bunting	*Emberiza melanocephala*						
PM, RB, WV	Corn Bunting	*Miliaria calandra*						

MAMMALS

English name	Scientific name							
Eastern Hedgehog	*Erinaceus concolor*							
Greater white-toothed shrew	*Crocidura russula*							
Lesser Horseshoe bat	*Rhinolophus hipposideros*							
Greater Horseshoe bat	*Rhinolophus ferrumequinum*							
Long-fingered bat	*Myotis capaccinii*							
Blasius Horseshoe bat	*Rhinolophus blasii*							
Geoffroy's bat	*Myotis emarginatus*							
Lesser Mouse-eared bat	*Myotis blythi*							
Serotine bat	*Eptesicus serotinus*							
Common Pipistrelle	*Pipistrellus pipistrellus*							
Kuhl's Pipistrelle	*Pipistrellus kuhli*							
Savi's Pipistrelle	*Pipistrellus savii*							
Grey long-eared bat	*Plecotus austriacus*							
Schreiber's bat	*Miniopterus schreibersii*							
Free-tailed bat	*Tadarida teniotis*							
Rabbit	*Oryctolagus cuniculus*							
Brown Hare	*Lepus capensis*							
Fat Dormouse	*Glis glis*							
Ship Rat	*Rattus rattus*							
Wood Mouse	*Apodemus sylvaticus*							
Rock Mouse	*Apodemus mystacinus*							
House Mouse	*Mus musculus*							
Cretan Spiny Mouse	*Acomys cahirinus*							
Weasel	*Mustela nivalis*							
Beech Marten	*Martes fiona*							
Badger	*Meles meles*							
Monk Seal	*Monachus monachus?*							
Wild Goat	*Capra aegagrus*							
Killer Whale	*Orcinus orca*							
Bottle-nosed Dolphin	*Tursiops truncatus*							
Risso's Dolphin	*Grampus griseus*							
Rough-toothed Dolphin	*Stero bredanensis*							
False Killer Whale	*Pseudorca crassideris* Rare							
Common Dolphin	*Delphinus delphis*							
Striped Dolphin	*Stenella coeruleoalbus* Rare							
Porpoise	*Phocoena phocoena* Rare							

AMPHIBIANS and REPTILES

English name	Scientific name							
Green Toad	*Bufo viridis*							
Common Tree Frog	*Hyla arborea*							
Marsh Frog								
	Rana ridibunda							
Stripe-necked Terrapin	*Mauremys caspica*							
Loggerhead Turtle	*Caretta caretta*							
Moorish Gecko	*Tarentola mauritanica*							
Turkish Gecko	*Hemidactylus turcicus*							
Kotschy's Gecko	*Cyrtodactylus kotschyi*							
Mediterranean Chameleon	*Chamaeleo chamaeleon*							
Balkan Green Lizard	*Lacerta trilineata*							
Erhard's Wall Lizard	*Podarcis erhardii*							
Ocellated Skink	*Chalcides ocellatus*							
Balkan Whip Snake	*Coluber gemonensis*							
Leopard Snake	*Elaphe situla*							
Dice Snake	*Natrix tessellata*							
Cat Snake	*Telescopus fallax*							

BUTTERFLIES

English name	Scientific name							
Papilionidae								
Swallowtail	*Papilio machaon*							
Scarce Swallowtail	*Iphiclides podalirius*							
Southern Festoon	*Zerynthia polyxena*							
Eastern Festoon	*Z. cerisyi (pale Cretan form) f. cretica*							
Pieridae								
Large White	*P. brassicae*							
Small White	*Artogeia rapea*							
Mountain Small White	*A. ergane*							
Bath White	*Pontia daplidice*							
Dappled White	*Euchloe simplonia*							
Gruner's Orange Tip	*Anthocharis gruneri*							
Clouded Yellow	*Colias croce*							
Brimstone	*Gonepteryx rhamni*							
Cleopatra	*G. cleopatra*							
Powdered Brimstone	*G. farinosa*							
Wood White	*Leptidea sinapis*							
Danaidae								
Plain Tiger	*Danaus chryippas*							
Libytheidae								
Nettle Tree	*Libythea celtis*							
Nymphalidae								
Two tailed Pasha	*Charaxes jasius*							
Large Tortoiseshell	*Nymphalis polychloris*							
Small Tortoiseshell	*Aglais urticae*							
Comma	*Polygonia c-album*							
Southern Comma	*P. egea*							
Painted Lady	*Vanessa cardui*							
Red Admiral	*Vanessa atalanta*							
Cardinal	*Pandoriania pandora*							
Queen of Spain	*Issoria lathonia*							
Satyridae								
Balkan Marbled White	*Melanargia larissa*							
Cretan Grayling	*Hipparchia semele cretica*							
The Hermit	*Chazara briseis*							
White-banded Grayling	*Pseudochazara anthelea*							
Great Banded Grayling	*Brintesia circe*							
Meadow Brown	*Maniola jurtina*							
Oriental Meadow Brown	*M. lupina*							
Cretan Small Heath	*C. pamphilus thynsis*							
Speckled Wood	*Pararge aergeria*							
Wall Brown	*Lasiommata megera*							

English name	Scientific name							
Lycaenidae								
Small Copper	*Lycaena phlaeas*							
Long-tailed Blue	*Lampides boeticus*							
Lang's Short-tailed Blue	*Syntarucus pirithous*							
African Grass Blue	*Zizeeria knysna*							
Small Blue	*Cupido minimus*							
Osiris Blue	*Cupido osiris*							
Baton Blue	*Pseudophilotes baton*							
Holly Blue	*Celastrina argiolus*							
Grass Jewel	*Freyeria trochylus*							
Silver-studded Blue	*Plebejus argus*							
Cretan Argus	*Kretania psylorita*							
Brown Argus	*Aricia agestis*							
Common Blue	*Polyommatus icarus*							
Hesperidae								
Oberthur's Grizzled Skipper	*P. armoricanus*							
Mallow Skipper	*Carcharodus alceae*							
Lulworth Skipper	*Thymelicus acteon*							
Essex Skipper	*T. lineola*							
Small Skipper	*T. flavus*							
Mediterranean Skipper	*Gegenes nostradamus*							
Pygmy Skipper	*G. pumilo*							

LATE RECEIVED ADDITIONAL RECORDS

Leach's Storm Petrel *Oceanodroma leucorrhao*
Vagrant 1 record
1984 An acoustic record of a bird flying inland from the sea at dusk, at Hersonissos 27.4.1984. (K. Mauer).

Black-shouldered Kite *Elanus caeruleus*
Vagrant 1 record
1987 1 adult above the old village of Aghia Triada, Messera Plain on the evening of 14.12.1987. (C. Vagliano). 1st record for Greece and Crete.

White-tailed Eagle *Haliaeetus albicilla*
Vagrant 2 records
1977 1 adult on Dikti Mt. Lassithi 26.3.-16.4. 1977. (Wilde 1980).
1989 1 2nd year immature on Rodopos Peninsula 17.3.1989. (B. Hallman).

Lesser Spotted Eagle *Aquila pomarina*
Vagrant 3 records
1967 1 Anogia early September (R. Koch in Bauer et. al.).
1974 1 immature on Dragonada 14.10.1974. (Crete Ringing Group).
1992 One recovery of a nestling ringed in Czechslovakia. Ringed 22.7.1992 at Orava, Dolny Kubin, Slovakia. Recovered at Heraklion 30.10.1992. It had travelled 1667 km and lived 100 days.

Spotted Eagle *Aquila clanga*
Vagrant
1988 1 immature in the mountains S. of Sitia 17.9.1988. (W. Scharlau).

Imperial Eagle *Aquila heliaca*
Vagrant 3 records
1967 1 adult at Kournas 19.4.1976. (J. Anderson).
1985 1 immature near Ierapetra late April or early May 1985. (P. Bray).
1986 1 immature N. of Omalos plateau 22.4.1986. (A. Vittery).

Long-toed Stint *Calidris subminuta*
Vagrant 1 record
1991 1 in winter plumage photographed at Vai on 28.3.1991. (A. Gosler, C.M. Jackson-Houlston & P. Grundy) 1st record for Greece and Crete.

Spotted Sandpiper *Actitis macularia*
Vagrant 1 record
1992 1 adult on Spinalonga island on 11.5.1992. (B. Lee).
1st record for Greece and Crete.

Great Skua *Stercorarius skua*
Vagrant
1993 1 off Sitia on 19.10.1993. (R. Grimmond).

Oriental Turtle Dove *Streptopelia orietalis*
Vagrant
1986 1 near the monastery of Aghia Triada on 27.4.1986. (A. Vittery).

Laughing Dove *Streptopelia senegalensis*
Vagrant
1983 1 near Aghia Galini 5.9.1982. (no details).

Waxwing *Bombycilla garrulus*
Vagrant
At last 10 shot and a few more seen in cages in Heraklion in early March 1966 (data from a hunters magazine).

Paddyfield Warbler *Acrocephalus agricola*
Vagrant 1 record
1969 1 at Almyros, Georgioupolis 16.4.1969. (M. Hodge).
1st and only record for Greece. (Handrinos 1994).

Spotless Starling *Sturnus unicolor*
Vagrant 1 record
1967 1? at Geropotamos river in May 1967. (Bauer et. al. 1969).

Crag Martins